The Heart of The Matter

By

Shirley M. Starr

and

Lori L. Waltemyer

Starr Publications
Red Lion PA

ISBN 0-9728162-1-6

First Printing June, 2003

NOTE: All verses taken from the Authorized Version (KJV).

Printed in the U.S.A. by
Morris Publishing
3212 East Highway 30
Kearney, NE 68847
1-800-650-7888

Dedication

This book is dedicated to all of the faithful ladies of Mt. Zion Baptist Church in Brogue, Pennsylvania who have patiently absorbed and applied the Scriptural teachings of this most difficult topic. Thank you for your precious love and ongoing encouragement.

Preface

In a day of eroding values, broken homes, and moral decay, God's never-changing Word still calls us to return to the old paths, the ancient landmarks. "Thus saith the Lord, Stand ye in the ways, and see, and ask for the old paths, where is the good way, and walk therein, and ye shall find rest for your souls..." *(Jer. 6:16a)* "Remove not the ancient landmark, which thy fathers have set." *(Prov. 22:28)*

However, past generations have been as stubborn as the Israelites were, refusing to follow godly principles. Are we like the Israelites, saying to God, "We will not walk therein?" *(Jer. 6:16b)*

Our desire, through this booklet, is to share what the Lord says through His word about our appearance as godly women. What should we wear? How should we look? Whom should we please? We are pulled in so many directions by the fashions of the day and by the views of our families and friends that we often do not even know what the Word of God teaches about dress.

The Bible gives definite guidelines to us as Christian ladies on dress and appearance. We belong to the King of Kings. We are his princesses and should dress to please the King. The key question is—Are we willing to follow what the Bible says?

We are excited to share these Biblical guidelines with you in the hope that we will all be a pleasing pattern of our Lord and Saviour, Jesus Christ. Let's re-stake the ancient landmark and walk in the old paths!

Foreword

More than—**just a rule**

In many churches, a dress code is **just the rule**. In my experience, people have said to me, "You probably dress like that because you're the pastor's wife." Interestingly enough, my husband never told me I had to dress a certain way. He often complimented me when I wore a dress, but he let God work on my heart.

After having my second child in 1975, I could not get into my pair of pants. It discouraged me greatly. I decided at that time to get rid of my pants, but more for convenience sake. After all, the pants did not fit and I had no money to buy more! Upon getting rid of them, the Lord miraculously supplied many dresses and skirts through a garage and yard sale my mother-in-law was having. She knew nothing about my decision.

In 1975 as a staff member in our Christian School, I was required to abide by the dress code. It was **just the rule**. In 1977, my husband began pursuing his master's degree. His college handbook stated that no student or student's wife was to be seen outside of her own home in slacks. No reason was given: it was **just the rule**. I abided by the rule, but did not know why. Shortly after this, I picked up the book entitled, *Your Clothes Say It For You.* The principles discussed therein really caused me to start thinking about my own personal standard of dress.

The Lord called my husband to pastor a small country church in Pennsylvania in 1990. He asked me to teach a class to the ladies on dress. I nearly panicked! What did I know about it? It was **just the rule**! I began digging into God's Word and looking for books on the matter. Much to my surprise, there were hardly any books written. No one wanted to touch the topic.

As I studied God's Word, He began to convict my own heart and teach me many things from the Scriptures which confirmed the stand I had maintained, but did not know why. **Now it was in my heart** from the Scriptures and **not just a rule**.

We have had ladies classes at our church every year since 1991 and every year God has strengthened my own stand of dress as I teach the principles found in His Word. It has been a joy to watch Him work on ladies in His timing and His way with His Word to change their **hearts** about this controversial issue.

As you explore ***Dress--The Heart of the Matter***, may **your** code of dress become a conviction, too, and not **just a rule**!

Shirley Starr

Rules, rules, and more rules

During my childhood years (late 1960's-1981), I grew up in a Christian home and a church that taught that women should wear dresses and skirts. The church spoke much regarding the issue of modesty; however, I cannot remember them instructing us at all in the principle of identification. Though modesty was taught, it was not thoroughly explained in the light of the Biblical principles that you will read in this book.

Consequently, no one seemed to obey **the *church's* rules** of dress. I stress that it was **the church's rule**, because it never became **my rule** until around 1992. Though we all wore dresses to church and had no problem with it, most of the people that I remember wore pants within the confines of their own homes. In fact, we wore pants to everything except church. I wore pants for school, work, play, and even church activities for the most part. I hated dressing up. I was a tomboy through and through.

Growing up in the country with a neighborhood of boys, I played tackle football and baseball, went biking, swimming, sledding, ice skating, roller skating, and participated in all sorts of sporty activities. I loved being able to keep up with the boys and prided myself on the fact that there were no boys that could outrun or outplay me, until my teenage years (even then I made sure that I gave them some hearty competition). I loved to win and hated defeat. Recesses and track and field days found me in the glory of healthy competition. I believed that my life was not conducive to *girlie dresses*.

In my teenage years, I gave up being a tomboy. Though I still loved the outdoors, I was not quite as rough-and-tumble as previously. Nevertheless, I was not about to give up my skin-tight blue jeans for a pair of culottes or a dress. The few people in our church who did wear culottes were not a lot of help to me. I thought that they looked sloppy and thoroughly ridiculous. My attitude was that I would never allow myself to look that sloppy or unfashionable. I started to develop an interest in fashion and at one point even considered fashion design as a career.

While living at home, we used to listen to Christian radio broadcasts. The majority of them were good, though I realize today that many of them leaned toward New Evangelicalism. On one of those broadcasts I heard a preacher talking about the pants issue. He made the following comment, "There is a difference between men and women's pants. You wouldn't catch a real man dead in a pair of women's slacks. There are many activities in which it is more modest for a woman to wear a pair of pants than a dress." That may not be word for word, but he cemented the issue in my mind. I guess that I was too young and gullible to look into the Bible to see what God had to say about the issue. Plus, that preacher said precisely what I wanted to hear. As far as I was concerned, that was the end of the discussion—case closed.

Fortunately, God in His mercy made sure that the case was reopened. For the most part, I lived in my britches until my late twenties when I began attending a small country church in southern Pennsylvania with my husband. I knew that their dress standards were similar to the church that I had attended in my childhood; however, that did not bother me. I knew there were also people in that church who did not adhere to the dress standards outside of church, so I figured that I was *safe*. However, the Lord started burdening my heart about my lack of surrender to His will in the area of dress.

At the time, I was employed at a bank which had a dress standard for its employees. We were required to wear dresses or dress suits at work for a professional look. I worked four to five days a week; therefore, I wore a dress the majority of the time. It was **the rule**, and I adhered to it. The Lord convicted me about the fact that if I would conform to a standard of dress for a job, why would I not conform to His standards of dress in obedience to His commands?

Because of my stubbornness, it took some wrestling with Him; nevertheless, I finally surrendered to His will. I cannot say that I understood all the principles of His Word regarding dress as I do today. Yet, I knew that if I were going to do anything for God, I would have to surrender my dress to Him. That is not to mention the fact that the Lord had given us a beautiful little daughter whom I wanted to raise for the Lord Jesus Christ. I did not want to teach her a double standard of hypocrisy. I did not want her thinking that she could pick and choose the principles of God that she wanted to obey. I wanted her to obey all of God's principles. Accordingly, I must obey them and be an example to her; therefore, I submitted to God's plan.

Obedience to **God's rules** of dress brings such blessing and peace to your life. There is no activity that I did in the past that I cannot do today in a dress or culottes. We go sledding in them, hike in them, bowl in them, horseback ride in them, lift weights in them, and yes, we even swim in them. There is no reason that is suitable to God to bear your body in an immodest fashion before the world. No reason!!!

As you read the principles in this book, **open your heart** to God and allow Him to teach you His ways which are always best. When you consider His sacrifice for you on the cross, is it really so terribly difficult to obey His Word by ridding yourself of the things in your life that displease Him? Remember His complete, selfless sacrifice for you. Open your will to ***The Heart of the Matter*** concerning ***Dress***!

Lori Waltemyer

Table of Contents

Dress—The Heart of The Matter

Chapter 1

HISTORY
"The Heart of the Past"

What has influenced women's dress through the years? History clearly shows that social, economic, and political forces definitely affected ladies' fashions. Sadly enough, the Word of God apparently was never taken into consideration by designers or salespeople. Like today, a vast majority of women followed the trends of the times, becoming enslaved to look like and to purchase the latest fashion of the day.

The Beginning

Fig leaves were the first materials used for clothing as Genesis 3:7 states. From the very beginning of time, there was a clothing problem. After sinning, Adam and Eve realized they were naked and made themselves aprons out of fig leaves. The Hebrew word for apron (*chagorah*) means a "belt for the waist, or a girdle." These aprons did not meet God's standard of covering, so the Lord became the first tailor and made coats for them out of animal skins "and clothed them." *(Gen. 3:21)* The Hebrew word for coat (*kuttoneth*) means "to cover or to clothe, a garment, or a robe." Notice here the distinction between the apron not covering the upper body and the fact that the robe covered **all** from the shoulders and downward. Man's ways were not good enough to cover his nakedness from the sin he had committed.

Throughout Bible days, the people wore three basic pieces of clothing. The **tunic** was a long under-dress having sleeves and reaching to the ankles. *(Song 5:3)* Men wore their tunics slightly shorter than women. The second piece of clothing was the **girdle, or belt**. It wrapped around the tunic at the waist and was frequently made of leather or coarse cloth. Often, women studded their girdles with precious stones and wore them slightly lower and more loosely than men. The third garment was the **cloak**, a long robe worn on top of the tunic. This robe was worn mainly for warmth. At night, the people would remove their cloak and girdle and sleep in their tunics.

During times of work or battle, the men would "gird up their loins," tying the robe up in order to run and fight. The priests were commanded to wear linen breeches beneath their robes to cover their nakedness when they offered sacrifices. *(Exod. 28:42)*

Throughout the early years, people continued to use animal skins, wool, hair, and linen cloth made from flax for their clothing needs.

1000-1900 A.D.

In the year 1000, the spinning wheel, a device for weaving, was invented in India and China, facilitating the production of yarn or thread. From 1225-1500, several happenings occurred which expedited the production of clothing. Cotton manufacturing began in Spain; lace making started; knitting commenced in England; and the shirt was developed. 1567 boasted the year of the first pair of jeans worn by sailors in Italy.

By 1733, the flying shuttle was patented in England enhancing the production of woven cloth. Other inventions such as the spinning Jenny, steam-powered loom, cloth-stitching machine, and waterproof fabric served to affect clothing production up through the year 1819.

In 1848, a bathing dress was designed for women with wide sleeves and big skirts. Levi Strauss invented modern jeans from tent fabric dyed blue in 1850 and Isaac Singer produced the treadle-powered sewing machine in 1851, selling them from door to door. Also during this time, Amelia Bloomer introduced the first trousers for women, called bloomers "featuring pants worn under a skirt." This created no small stir when she wore them in public.

1900-1920

The 1900's began the most rapid fashion changes in America. Some of this was due to the postal service beginning rural delivery. The average American woman could now see the latest styles because of "mass circulation magazines, pattern catalogs, and mail order catalogs."

Gaining the right to vote and entering the work force affected the role of women as well as their dress. By 1910, 7,500,000 women had jobs outside of the home. It was also at this time that the U.S. began to manufacture rayon, the staple fabric for stockings and dresses. In just four short years, the women in the work force had increased to 8,500,000, many of them in garment factories.

1914-1918 were the years of World War I. Women took on more new roles in factories and offices and **began to wear pants**. Clothing became more relaxed with a tubular look and less flowing. Things perceived as **sinful** before the war, like short hair and trousers for women were thought to be **practical** for war work. This is pragmatism without regard to what God says. Still most women continued to wear dresses in their homes.

By 1917, some women even entered the armed forces. They wore a variety of uniforms. Colors were drab and clothes were practical due to dye and fabric shortages.

1920-1930

In the early 1920's, pants were worn only by lady campers and hikers with a more casual look prevailing. Young people questioned the older generation's values. With the trend leaning toward youth, women started dieting to obtain a flatter teenage shape and morals declined also. A 1920 article stated that the **purpose of clothing was to cover and provide protection,** but that people now had a new burden of impressing others and showing their ability to spend money, with **the current trend being one "to reveal."** It seems that tight pants were a problem even then as the author stated that in previous years "comfortable trousers would not be discarded in favor of tight ones that must be got into with the aid of a shoe horn and talcum powder." (*Saturday Evening Post,* June 26, 1920, p. 165)

Women were experiencing what they thought was more freedom. They became more involved in sports and were called "flappers," – meaning "a young woman showing freedom from convention." Smoking, public drinking, and more sensual, alluring clothing were the rage of the day. The alluring clothing was used to catch a fellow as there was a shortage of men due to the war. Women adopted trousers and bared their legs in public during those "Roaring Twenties."

In the late 20's the idea of pants had taken a universal hold **with the emergence of shorts**, which was the next step from short skirts and a desire to dress like a young boy.

1930-1940

The Great Depression influenced this decade. The number of women working decreased. Women desired to return to a more feminine image as they returned to their homes. Movies abounded with women imitating fashions of the movie stars. Hollywood set the fashion trends of the day. Dress lengths dropped.

America would send buyers and designers to Paris to discover the latest fashions. If a lady bought a dress said to be inspired from Paris, it was worth more to her psychologically and to the seller financially. A French model might wear a copied dress designed in Hollywood and it would bring a high price. The motto was: "Make the customer happy!" American women would pay for the foreign label!

In 1933, a woman named Alice Marble first wore shorts during a tennis match in Wimbledon, England.

In 1940, college girls began wearing men's clothing, a fad that had been growing since World War I. Slacks and shorts became more popular and were thought to be a "revulsion" or rebellion against grandma's bustles and hoopskirts. Fashion designers forecasted that within ten years, ladies would be wearing trousers not only to play in, but also for work. They were right!

1940-1950

This decade brought World War II and the designing of women's work clothing by the Bureau of Home Economics and the U.S. Department of Agriculture. These clothes consisted of one-piece mechanics suits and coverettes for farm women. The coverettes were like cover-alls, but the name made them sound feminine.

By 1942, women quickly took to the wearing of pants and the episode was predicted to escalate. The War Production Boards passed a law, Order L-85, limiting the amount of material that could go into a gown, creating shorter hemlines and narrower skirts. Slacks on women moved from the sports category to all areas of activity. Sales increased ten times and dress designers modified new styles to include some version of pants. One authority stated that "the theft of each masculine garment symbolized a further step in women's progress." (*NY Times Magazine,* March 1, 1942, p. 16)

Pants were worn mainly as a matter of comfort. The argument was that ladies did not have to worry about pulling their skirt down or being warm, plus they saved money on stockings, laundry, and dry cleaning. (Pragmatism again!)

To make women feel more comfortable about the pants issue, *Vogue* magazine introduced "A Primer on Pants," – when to wear them, how to wear them, and how to buy them. However, to pacify the conservatives and those resisting change, they also stated " . . . a skirt is never wrong." (*Time,* April 13, 1942, pp. 18-19) Skirts still dominated the picture!

In 1943, The National Catholic Women's Organization spoke out angrily against the fashions of the day. They proclaimed that the immodest dress of the day was against the sixth and ninth commandments, and that only corrupt minds would contribute to the moral decay. The pope urged Catholic women to "dress decently at all times," and to avoid public beaches where people were scantily dressed. Wow!

Two years prior to this outcry, Pope Pius XII warned girls against the fashions. He said that though some dresses might be more comfortable, if they proved "dangerous for the soul, they must be unfailingly rejected." (*Newsweek,* September 6, 1943, p. 90) Adamantly opposing guidelines set by the War Production Board, the Catholic Church rejected the V-neck dress thought to be a "morale-builder" for the servicemen.

In 1944, Rudofsky, a Moravian, arranged an art exhibit at The Museum of Modern Art. He said, "The modern tendency in dress is toward elimination (i.e. taking clothes off). Man seeks comfort: the young woman seeks attention." (*Newsweek,* December 11, 1944, p. 102)

Once Paris was liberated from Germany in 1944, clothing designers were excited to see what new fashions would appear. During this time, France boasted that a million people indirectly lived on their fashion industry and that they could export $400,000,000 worth of fashions. The clothing designs appeared "mannish" and "arrogant." Though women leaned toward a more feminine look, they also had a desire for luxury after the years of sacrifice and rationing during the war.

Marlene Dietrich and Katherine Hepburn popularized wearing trousers in public. Camisoles were developed to replace slips (underskirts) as women now regularly wore pants.

Morals continued to decline as Louis Reard from France introduced the bikini bathing suit in 1946. Christian Dior revived the Paris fashion center encouraging long narrow skirts accentuating the figure in 1947.

In 1949, **slit-skirts** made their appearance with slits shown in the back or up the side from 4-9 inches long. The highlight of this style was a short glimpse of the upper calf and knee.

1950-Present

The 50's introduced pantyhose, saddle shoes, and the steam iron. Women were becoming bolder and more aggressive in their public dress as evidenced by the following episode.

Congressmen from the House became upset over a lady wearing shorts into the visitor's gallery. They reasoned that she "impaired the dignity of the House and distracted its members." (*Newsweek,* September 1, 1955, p. 29) They then proceeded to ban anyone over the age of ten in shorts to enter the gallery.

The Senate did not agree. Several women, outraged by the issue, complained to their Congressmen that their constitutional rights were being violated, so the House reversed the order.

In 1956 a village in Southampton, Long Island, seeking to preserve its dignity, prevented people from wearing immodest apparel. It was an uphill battle.

The early 60's ushered in Mary Quant from London, "the most influential 1960's designer." She designed the mini-skirt and hot pants. The mini-skirt necessitated the invention of pantyhose and the wearing of boots for women.

The mid-60's brought political and social revolution in schools and colleges throughout America. The three primary movements dominating this period were the Civil Rights movement, the Vietnam War, and the Women's Lib movement. As a result of these, revolutionary clothing appeared with see-through blouses, no bras, topless bathing suits, the maxi-coat, etc. Morality hit an all time low and pantsuits were now popular in professional and formal situations.

Fashion designs arose from the streets and were no longer dictated by French designers. Rock music influenced clothing also with bell-bottoms, psychedelic prints, wild colors, vinyl and cellophane dresses, go-go boots, and ruffled shirts for men.

The trend has been one of decline ever since with pantsuits, and formfitting dresses in the 70's. Until this period, "it was not fashionable and sometimes against the law to wear pants in offices, classrooms, and restaurants in the U.S." (www.Factmonster.com) This author remembers not being allowed to wear pants in High School classes through graduation in 1969! "Streaking," or running naked in public became a fad during this period of time.

Designer jeans were made popular in the 80's with people paying any price for the brand name. One website quotes, "jeans were the first trousers to put women and men on equal terms." (www.Factmonster.com) Feminism abounded with militant feminists denying motherhood and accepting homosexuality by the use of "manipulation, domination, and intimidation." (www.leadingtheway.org) With feminism becoming the opposite of femininity, wouldn't the clothing also change to reflect that contrast?

The 90's fashion motto was "anything goes," and it has been "anything goes" ever since. What a sad commentary on America is the history of the dress of its women!

Concluding this chapter, we see how clothing was and is directly influenced by social, economic, and political factors. History has clearly reflected this through the ages. In 1943, the Catholic Church was outraged by the decline in women's dress, but today, not even our Bible-believing churches are outraged. In 1955, the U.S. House of Representatives recognized that a woman in shorts was improper and distracting. Today, we Bible-believers have lost that sense of propriety, morality, and conscience.

It is not only America that is guilty of decline in the area of women's dress. If we are honest, we have to admit that the culture has triggered a decline in the church, too. Instead of the church impacting the culture, the culture has impacted the church. However, as Christian ambassadors, we have a higher influence guiding our choice of clothing. We have definite Biblical guidelines to follow.

Suggested Assignment

Think about the fashion trends that you have seen in your lifetime. Can you remember the days when women mainly wore dresses? If possible, ask your mother and grandmother about the fashion trends of their day. Notice how things have declined from God's view of dress.

Notes

Chapter 2

SEPARATION

"The Heart of Holiness"

Where has preaching on the doctrine of separation gone through the years? Though today's Christians seem to avoid and disdain the issue, God Almighty has commanded the separation of the believer from that which is unholy and impure. It is clearly taught and required in Scripture by a holy God Who cannot look on sin and finds no pleasure in it. He has written and plainly defined in His word definite guidelines of separation that must be followed in order to lead a holy and pure life before Him. Follow along as we discuss separation, "the heart of holiness."

The Definition

The word separate means "to disunite, to divide, to sever, or to part things naturally or casually joined." *(Webster's 1828 Dictionary)* Believers in Christ are expected by God to divide themselves, or sever, from all that is unholy and unrighteous in His eyes. Just as a stonewall divides one property from another, the Lord requires His children to divide themselves from every form of evil, whether it be theft, murder, drunkenness, or even improper attire.

The Doctrine

Through the act of creation in Genesis 1:4, 6-7, the principle of separation is first mentioned and clearly set forth. One of God's first transactions in creation was to make light. When God saw the light, He saw that it was good; therefore, He divided the light from the darkness. Even in creation, He desired that the two be separate from one another. Certainly, it can be argued that this passage is speaking of creation; nevertheless, it is a principle that God is setting forth through His creation. He desires that light and darkness be separate. God considered the light good; darkness is linked to that which is without form and void. Light represents goodness and purity; whereas, darkness symbolizes evil and degradation. It is no coincidence that thieves, murderers, drug addicts, and drunkards generally perform their evil acts in the darkness of the night. Evil thrives upon darkness.

In stark contrast, Jesus Christ is the light of the world. *(John 1:9; 3:19; 8:12)* He is the epitome of all that is good, holy, and righteous, for He is God incarnate. In light of the fact that believers are His children, He requires them to separate themselves from the darkness of sin in whatever form that it may take. Christ declared Christians to be lights to those around them. *(Matt. 5:14-16; Eph. 5:8; 1 Thess. 5:5)* However, sin and a lack of separation dims that light and causes darkness to dominate. If the believer refuses to be a light to this present world, who then will be that light?

In Genesis 1:6-7, God divided the waters from the waters by the firmament. Throughout the Bible and especially in the book of Revelation, water is representative of people and nations. *(Rev. 17:15)* The firmament is represented by the cross. Over 2000 years ago, the cross of Christ divided those who accept Him as Savior from those who reject Him. It was the only part of creation that God did not say was good. God did not want Jesus to die on the cross, but man's sinfulness and rebellion necessitated it. God is holy and cannot look on sin. He also commands the believer to be holy and separate.

The Division

In Genesis, God separated men and women to do His work. He separated Noah to build the ark. He separated Abraham from Lot, a carnal Christian. God also separated the children of Israel from the rest of the world. Exodus 8:23 declares, "And I will put a division between my people and thy people." The Lord wanted the Israelites to know that there was a difference between them and the Egyptians. *(Exod. 11:7)* In fact, it was Israel's desire to be like all the other nations that continually caused trouble for them. God made them His special, chosen people. He bestowed light upon them and eventually rescued them from the bondage of Egypt, yet they longed to return to the darkness and bondage of sin. Christians are too often like Israel! Christ has rescued believers from the bondage of sin and has given them the light of truth; however, believers frequently desire to depart from God's light and return to the bondage and darkness of sin. They long to look like, talk like, act like, and smell like this present world. This carnal pattern reveals a lack of desire to separate and live a holy life before God and the world.

In Numbers 6, God required the Nazarites to separate themselves unto Him. When either a man or a woman took a Nazarite vow, they were to separate themselves from strong drink, the razor, and dead bodies. Numbers 6:8 states, "All the days of his separation he is holy unto the Lord." The Nazarite was required before God to maintain a holy and pure life before Him.

The Levitical priests were also required to separate themselves unto the Lord. *(Num. 8:14-22)* In addition, separation is clearly taught throughout the Minor Prophets. Many of the Minor Prophets wrote to pronounce judgment on the Israelites for their lack of separation from the heathen around them. Daniel and the three Hebrew children separated themselves from the Babylonians and the king's meat. The book of Malachi declares God's love for Israel and Israel's refusal to separate themselves unto Him; therefore, God was forced to judge them for their sin through captivity and bondage to the heathen nations.

Separation is also clearly taught in the New Testament and is relevant to the present day believer. John the Baptist was a Nazarite who was separated unto God even before his birth. *(Luke 1:15)* God knows each and every person before birth. *(Psa. 139)* He expects His born again children to separate themselves unto Him and live holy lives.

Paul and Barnabas were separated by God for the work of the ministry. Indeed, they were called of God to preach the gospel, yet holiness is demanded of all believers as shown in 2 Corinthians 6:14-18 where God makes separation a command and applicable to all of His present day children. This passage boldly commands:

> **"Be ye not unequally yoked together with unbelievers: for what fellowship hath righteousness with unrighteousness? and what communion hath light with darkness?**
>
> And what concord hath Christ with Belial? or what part hath he that believeth with an infidel?
>
> And what agreement hath the temple of God with idols? for ye are the temple of the living God; as God hath said, I will dwell in them, and walk in *them*; and I will be their God, and they shall be my people.
>
> **Wherefore come out from among them, and be ye separate, saith the Lord, and touch not the unclean *thing*; and I will receive you,**
>
> And will be a Father unto you, and ye shall be my sons and daughters, saith the Lord Almighty."

Possibly, believers could try to explain away the separation of the Nazarites or the Levitical priests. Maybe they could even make excuses why they believe that Israel's separation was different from that of the New Testament believer, *though the principle still remains.* However, 2 Corinthians 6:14-18 cannot be revoked. Paul, through the inspiration of the Holy Spirit, was speaking to the common, ordinary New Testament believer like you and me. If believers refuse to separate from that which is unholy, they reject the Bible and Christ and force Him to find them unacceptable.

Yes, the Bible makes it quite clear that there is to be a marked difference between the child of God and unbelievers.

The Demand

Just as 2 Corinthians 6 communicates the command for believers to separate, 1 Peter 1:16 also reveals His demand to be separate and holy. It pronounces, "Be ye holy; for I am holy." God is holy, and He expects the same from those who name His name. When believers refuse to live holy lives, they bring shame to God's holy name. Christ bought His children with His own precious blood; therefore, He has the right to expect them to live up to their name, Christian. And since Christian means "little Christ," He has every right to demand that believers live up to His holy name.

Purchasing something gives right of ownership. For example, those who purchase a car have the right to do whatever they desire with it. They have every right to expect it to perform and run to the best of its capability. The same is true of children and the family name. All people desire their children to carry on the family name with dignity and honor. Christ has the right to expect the same thing of Christians to an even higher degree.

The Duplicate

God has not left believers without an example in regard to separation and holiness. First of all, God is holy and righteous. *(Lev. 20:7)* Perhaps you are thinking, "Well, of course He is, but He is God." However, He sent His only Son, Jesus Christ, to this earth to live as a man for thirty-three and a half years. Jesus remained sinless and holy even in the midst of wicked men. He is the divine example of true holiness and separation. Hebrews 7:26 proclaims,

> "For such an high priest became us, *who* is holy, harmless, undefiled, separate from sinners, and made higher than the heavens;"

Jesus Christ set the ultimate example for believers to follow. He did not isolate Himself from sinners, but He did insulate Himself from evil and remained untouched by it. *(Vance Havner)* Separation and holiness is attainable in the believer's life.

The Design

Separation is a matter of holiness, the holiness of a heart that desires to be pure even as God is pure and holy. It is a matter of separating from evil, and it is a command by God to all believers. God requires holiness both internally and externally. He requires it of inward thoughts and attitudes. As well, He requires it of external actions such as refraining from fornication, from viewing pornography, from stealing, and even **from wearing fashions that displease Him**. The aim of all believers should be to please and glorify Christ. Holiness pleases Him and brings glory and honor to His righteous name. It presents Him properly before a sinful world. Certainly, holiness requires complete obedience to His just demands.

The Decision

Though separation and holiness are commanded by God both internally and externally, they can only be personally obtained by the conscious decision that a believer makes to follow God and His laws. Holiness cannot be spread or reproduced; it comes from the believer's decision to be holy with the help of the Holy Spirit because God requires it. It comes from a heart that desires to obey and please God. The Holy Spirit is sorely grieved when

He convicts the believer of sin and that believer refuses to separate from it. His voice of conviction grows fainter and fainter the longer that He is refused. This is a dangerous position for a child of God. Many times the carnal believer does not even recognize the terrible state of his heart and life. Such a state requires a return to God and an admission that holiness is the way that every believer should live.

Contrary to the way it is generally looked upon, separation is a positive aspect of the believer's life and walk. Though it demands the refusal of fleshly desires and ambitions, it brings tremendous blessing from the Lord, because God blesses those who obey Him. Deuteronomy 11:26-28 asserts,

> "Behold I set before you this day a blessing and a curse; A blessing, if ye obey the commandments of the LORD your God, which I command you this day: And a curse, if ye will not obey the commandments of the LORD your God, but turn aside out of the way which I command you this day, to go after other gods, which ye have not known."

Obedience brings blessing, but disobedience brings a curse. God lays out clear commands in His Word that He expects the believer to obey.

John Brown, a nineteenth century Scottish theologian, stated that holiness "consists in thinking as God thinks, and willing as God wills." Too often believers like the way that they think and have no desire to change their thinking to meet God's standards of holiness. In refusing to change, they curse themselves and their families. The decision rests upon each individual believer whether to obey and follow God or live life according to this world's limited understanding.

God gives definite guidelines in His Word with regard to dress. Will you open your heart to see His principles and apply them to your life? Joshua 24:15 aptly proclaims,

> "And if it seem evil unto you to serve the LORD, **choose you this day whom ye will serve;** whether the gods which your fathers served that *were* on the other side of the flood, or the gods of the Amorites, in whose land ye dwell: but **as for me and my house, we will serve the LORD."**

Whom will you choose to serve in your life and dress? Will you choose to proclaim, as Joshua, "I will serve the Lord?"

Suggested Assignment

Pray and ask God to give you an open mind and an open heart concerning the Biblical principles of dress to be discussed in the remaining chapters of this book.

Chapter 3

MODESTY

"The Heart of Purity"

Modesty is an issue that most Christian ladies believe is firmly within their grasp. After all, they have little desire to parade around God's green earth half-dressed causing shame to themselves, their husbands and fathers, and their Lord. Most would affirm that God has given the command of modesty and are willing to comply in as much as they believe it to be a command. Modesty is considered a relatively "easy" area of obedience. However, it involves more than just the practice of refraining from wearing tight-fitting or low-cut clothing. There is more to the issue than that; therefore, let's analyze the heart of purity.

The Design

The goal of dress for every Christian woman must be two-fold. First, her aim should be to glorify God in her life. This must include her dress. 1 Corinthians 10:31 states,

> "Whether therefore ye eat, or drink, or **whatsoever ye do,** do all to the glory of God."

In this passage, Paul is addressing the fact that lawful acts do not always edify. He declares that he *could have done* as he pleased according to the law of conscience, yet there is a higher law – that of love which kept him from doing whatever he desired. He declares that though all things were lawful to him, all things were not expedient or edifying to himself or to others. In this passage of Scripture, Paul gives the guideline by which all Christians should live: ie., no matter what you do in life, do everything to the glory of God. This goal will keep you from sin. Do you as a godly, Christian lady think of glorifying Christ in all that you do? What about in regard to your dress? God made us to be females. Are we glorifying God in maintaining His order? Ask yourself in regard to everything that you wear, "Does my dress glorify God?" As you read this book, would you be willing to examine your dress honestly before God Almighty and change those areas that do not bring Him glory?

Secondly, the goal of the godly, Christian lady should be to maintain purity within herself and in others. 1 Corinthians 10:23-33 speaks of this issue. Paul declares that his love for others caused him to live differently than he *could have* lived. His goal was first to glorify God and, secondly, to offend no one. *(1 Cor. 10:33)* In other words, we are responsible for our lives before the world, ladies. Paul sought the profit of others that they should be saved. Whose profit are you seeking? Are you seeking to point others to Christ by your life, or are you seeking your own glory? The heart of purity in regard to dress really involves our pride, as all sin is a result of the pride of man against God's higher laws of truth. Are you willing to lay aside your pride (truly humble yourself), to glorify God, to edify other believers, and to point the unsaved to Christ for salvation?

The Demand

In 1 Timothy 2:9-10, God commands,

> "In like manner also, that women adorn themselves in **modest apparel, with shamefacedness and sobriety**; not with broided hair, or gold, or pearls, or costly array; But (which becometh women professing godliness) with good works."

Godly ladies are commanded by God to dress modestly. Maybe you are thinking, "No problem, I have that area of my life in subjection to Christ." Yet, if your practice is to wear pants, low necklines, tight clothes, short skirts, shorts, or bathing suits, you are not modest according to the Word of God! Let us examine God's command of modesty.

The Definition

The English word **modest** means **"properly restrained by a sense of propriety; hence, not forward or bold; not presumptuous or arrogant; not boastful."** The Christian lady is to refrain from wearing anything that is unrestrained, forward, bold, presumptuous, arrogant, and boastful. That includes a number of this world's fashions. Allow this author the privilege of escorting you down the runway to a sort of "fashion show" that presents an honest examination of some of this world's finery.

As you gaze down the fashion runway, the first item that dons our model is a white blouse and a pair of sleek black pants (they could be any color or variety). Think about what those pants represent – freedom from male domination, freedom to wear whatever a lady pleases, freedom to be sexy and casual, and the right to dress like the rest of the world. However, is that the godly lady's goal in dress?

Pants are thoroughly forward, bold, presumptuous, arrogant, and boastful. You can try to deny it, yet even the world of fashion describes pants as such. McCall's Magazine wrote an article several years ago entitled "What Your Intimate Behavior Says About You." According to Bruce Lackey in a sermon on dress, the article proclaimed that certain clothing are used as "sexual signaling devices" to attract male interest. In that article, the writer declared boldly and with brutal honesty that pants are worn to reveal the "primary genital zone." [sic] He wrote, "The first way to accentuate is to employ articles of clothing which underline the nature of the organ hidden beneath them. For the female, this means wearing trousers." (Cloud, *"O Timothy"*, Vol. 9, Issue 12, 1992 or see www.wayoflife.org) That particular writer was in no way condemning pants; in fact, he was telling ladies how to send sexual signals in their dress. He went on to state, "The way to emphasize the nature of the organs of the body is by wearing these clothing: trousers, shorts, or bathing costumes, that by their tightness reveal..."

Is wearing this type of clothing being properly restrained by a sense of propriety? Is it modest? Indeed not! Pants are designed to frame a woman's pelvic area (a tamer term for the genitals and buttocks), hips, and thighs. The seam of the pants encircles and draws attention to the entire area of the pelvis. Let us not pretend to be naïve, ladies. Most women like the attention that wearing pants brings them, not to mention the sense of authority that they feel by wearing them (remember from chapter 1, pants were the first item of clothing to place men and women on equal terms). The whistles and comments that men make all attest to the fact that pants are not modest apparel.

You may say, "Well that is one man's opinion of pants." Let us hear a woman's opinion of them and their purpose. Margaret Kent wrote a book entitled "How to Marry the Man of Your Choice." In it, she instructs women on how to manipulate men. In regard to pants she states, "jeans are likely to get a positive response because they are snug and outline the body; they also represent casualness." *(Kent, p. 36)* It is no coincidence that casual pants correspond with the day and age of casual sex.

In David Cloud's article on the issue, he made the following comment, "A woman in pants is either gross or sexually appealing, depending upon her figure." (fbns@wayoflife.org) In which category are you? Christian ladies that profess godliness belong in neither category! They are commanded by God to dress modestly. Modest apparel does not include pants. Not even *loose-fitting pants* are modest. They still frame the pelvic area. This is the area that God meant to be revealed only to your husband. Commercial advertisers capitalize on the fact that pants are tight, revealing, and sexy, although many Christian ladies will not admit it. It is ironic that Christian women deny what the world is freely willing to admit.

If the English word for modest does not convince you that pants are not considered modest apparel by God, let us discuss the Greek definition of the word, **modest,** in 1 Timothy 2:9. "**Katastole kosmios"** are the Greek words for "modest apparel" (Strong's Concordance - #2596, 2689, 2887, 4749). **Kata** is a preposition that means **down**; **stole** means **a long fitting gown, a stately robe reaching to the feet or a train sweeping to the ground. Kosmios** means **decently or orderly**. Thus, **katastole kosmios** means a **long, flowing garment that is let down decently.** Proper, modest dress is a mark of dignity on a woman.

When Paul wrote under the inspiration of the Holy Spirit that women should adorn themselves in modest apparel, he was speaking of a specific type of garment, not just a general description of what a woman should wear. God inspired Paul to tell ladies that they are to wear long, flowing garments that are let down decently. Are pants long, flowing garments? No, they are not. They are designed to be snug and formfitting. Even the bell-bottom trousers of the past were only flowing with material in the legs; otherwise, they were tight in all the *right* places (wrong according to God). Therefore, pants are automatically disqualified as modest apparel, because they are not long, flowing garments that are let down decently (not to mention the fact that they are distinctively man's apparel – see chapter 4 on Identification). They also do not meet God's definition of modesty.

Just as a properly fitting dress brings dignity to a woman, so pants bring them shame. They brand a woman as bossy, authoritative, and trying to "keep up with the men." Since the Garden of Eden, women have been struggling for authority and rank over men. Eve was deceived into believing that she could be like the gods *(Gen. 3*). What was she seeking? She sought equality and authority with God. Since that time, women have sought to rule over men. They think that pants give them that authority and equality. Each and every Christian lady would be offended if people said that she was the one who *wore the pants in the house*, yet many of them do both literally and figuratively.

Pants are a mark, brand, or decal on a woman that outwardly shows the inward condition of her heart. Just as long hair on a man is an outward sign of rebellion, so pants, shorts, and improper attire are that mark of rebellion on a woman.

God's design was for men and priests to wear pants. Their pants were called breeches in Bible times. *(Exod. 28:42-43; Lev. 6:10; Job 38:3; 40:7)* Today, they are called pants, trousers, slacks, or britches. No matter the name, they are still breeches, which were then and are still today designed specifically by God for the use of the male gender. He designed them to cover men from the loins to the thigh (see chapter 4 - Identification). Women did not wear them as late as 1910 and should not wear them today. Nor should women wear pantsuits, which are simply a spin-off of men's suits.

Just think, God was the first fashion Designer! Most of us would not argue with Christian Dior, Calvin Klein, or Liz Claiborne regarding fashions. Nevertheless, we will argue with God and tell Him that He does not know fashion when He created it and the rules pertaining to it. How silly we are to argue with our Creator! Once Christian ladies know the truth about dress, they must make a choice in regard to that truth. To reject God's truth is rebellion against an almighty God. To accept that truth brings God's blessing and fulfillment. What will you do with God's truth about dress?

The next item displayed in our fashion show wardrobe is a bright red sweater and a long, slender, navy skirt with a daring slit that extends to the middle of the thigh. How chic, sensual, and suggestive! However, is it modest? Does it show restraint by a sense of propriety? Or is it bold and forward? Of course, it is bold and forward! That is precisely how the fashion designers shape garments. The point is that modesty involves more than just wearing a dress. A woman can be indecently arrayed even in a dress or a skirt.

The godly lady's dresses and skirts are designed by God to be a long flowing garment that is let down decently; therefore, her clothing should not be tight or form-fitting. Her slits should extend no higher than the bottom of the kneecap, and her clothing should be a proper length.

But, what is considered a proper length? Who determines what is the proper length and when a slit is too high? Just as God designed that men should wear pants, He designed the long flowing garment for ladies and the proper length of that garment.

Wearing the hemline below the kneecap is the proper length for dresses or skirts. There needs to be enough material to cover your knees when you are sitting. Isaiah 47:1-3 gives insight as to what God considers nakedness or immodest dress lengths on women. In these verses, God is pronouncing judgment on Babylon because they are corrupt and are no longer tender and delicate. He specifically states what He considers nakedness. In verses 2-3, He says,

> "Take the millstones, and grind meal: uncover thy locks, **make bare the leg, uncover the thigh**, pass over the rivers. **Thy nakedness shall be uncovered, yea, thy shame shall be seen**: I will take vengeance, and I will not meet *thee as* a man."

God considers the baring of the thigh to be nakedness. The thigh (by definition) is the area that begins at the femur (hipbone) and ends at the patella (kneecap). If the thigh is uncovered, be it a man or a woman, God considers that person naked. The baring of the thigh is associated with harlotry. Therefore, short dresses, short skirts, shorts, and slits above the kneecap should not be worn by women professing godliness. Certainly, they do not bring glory to God. They draw attention to and bring glory to a woman's body. But, that is not the believer's goal in dress.

As the fashion show progresses, a model steps up onto the runway wearing a long, white, lacy, sweeping, V-neck dress fashioned with a delicate, sheer material. Now what could be unfeminine and bold about a dress like this? A low-cut neckline is not pleasing to God. Dresses and blouses must be moderate in the neckline in order for God to consider them modest. Godly ladies must be careful not to display their chests. When people look at you, their attention should be drawn to your face, not to the low V-neck or round-neck blouse or dress that shows the chest that only your husband should see. Many Christian ladies think that they are modestly dressed in their lovely church dress, yet some of those necklines are simply too low cut. It is hard to notice their face when they are standing there talking to you, let alone if they bend over to pick up their purse. A dress like that draws improper attention from others. It is embarrassing to other ladies and creates distracting, lustful images in the minds of men.

The V-neck was developed by designers solely for the purpose of drawing attention to a woman's chest. This type of neckline literally points down to a woman's breasts. It is like a giant arrow that screams out, "Look at what I have been endowed with." Ladies, our attire should glorify the Lord. He does not want us to draw attention to areas that are meant to be covered and only for our husband's pleasure (see Song of Solomon) and for breast-feeding our children. God meant for people to focus on our face, or our countenance, when they speak to and look at us. If we are drawing attention to our bodies, it is for our glory, not the Lord's. It is fleshly, carnal, devilish. A reasonable guideline for wearing rounded or V-neck apparel is that it be no lower than one to one and a half inches (two fingers) below the collarbone. Also, be sure that you are not revealing your chest or cleavage when you bend over. Beware of those gaping necklines!

Sheer, see-through clothing is not pleasing to God. It reveals what God has meant to be hidden since the fall of man in the Garden of Eden. Remember ladies that it is a shame to be naked. Be sure that you are wearing slips or white T-shirts under your clothes so that others cannot see through your skirts, blouses, and dresses. There are many attractive blouses available that are too sheer to wear with just your bra. If you wear them that way, others can see the color of your skin and bra through them. Nice blouses become immodest apparel when worn in that fashion. Remember to wear a slip for proper coverage.

The final merchandise in our fashion show is a pair of denim walking shorts with a hemline that falls three inches above the knee. The model is also adorned in a tight, pink lycra halter top. The crowd goes wild. How trendy, how lusty, how skimpy! Though shorts and halter-tops are the rave of the day, they are not to be the rave of godly ladies. Remember, ladies, that God wants our thighs covered. When God designed the coats in the Garden for Adam and Eve, He fashioned them to cover from their shoulders downward *(see Chapter 1- History, "The Beginning", p. 1)*. Displaying any part of your bosom, chest, and shoulders is nakedness to God. Even fashion designers describe the baring of the shoulders and back as soft, sexy, and alluring. This also includes bikinis and "modest" one-piece bathing suits. There are no modest bathing suits. They all bare the thigh and back. Bikinis also reveal the chest and bosom. Godly ladies are to be seen like that only by their husbands, certainly not by the whole church, office, or neighborhood. What we wear sends a message. Be sure that you are sending a godly message to a lost and dying world that is headed for hell and to the Christian world who needs an example to follow.

In 1 Timothy 2:9, Paul urges Christian ladies to have shamefacedness and sobriety. Let us define these two words. **Shamefacedness** means **bashfulness or an excess of modesty.** In other words, godly ladies should be extra-modest. Unfortunately, there are too many women leaning toward excessive immodesty. Still others lean toward immodesty, but refuse to call it that, unwilling to accept the Scriptures and reasoning presented here. In God's sight, it is better to be too modest than to be too revealing.

Sobriety means **temperance; habitual freedom from enthusiasm, inordinate passion, or overheated imagination; calmness; or coolness**. It is high time that Christian ladies use temperance in their dress and bridle the inordinate passions that desire to receive the attention of men through their attire. It is much more profitable to receive the blessings of God than the whistles of men, not to mention the fact that beauty and good figures fade with time. If you build your self-confidence on those things, you are building on a crumbling foundation.

It is amazing to see an increasing number of middle age to older ladies trying to stay young and "cool" by their risque′ attire when they are supposed to be an example to teach the younger ladies godliness. Titus 2:3-4 says,

> "The aged women likewise, that *they be* in behaviour as becometh holiness, not false accusers, not given to much wine, teachers of good things; That they may teach the young women to be sober, to love their husbands, to love their children,

Ladies, let us be godly examples to others. God does not want young ladies parading around immodestly either. Let us teach our daughters to be godly ladies, not worldly ladies. It is imperative to begin this teaching early and not wait until they reach the teen years.

The Demise

Far too many Christian ladies seem unaware of their responsibility to the male population in regard to their garments. Women are not to wear things that cause men to look upon them and lust after them. It is easy to say that we are absolved of all responsibility in this area. Nevertheless, is that how God sees it? Are women responsible if men lust after them? God answers that question for us in Matthew 5:27-28 where He declares,

> "Ye have heard that it was said by them of old time, Thou shalt not commit adultery: But I say unto you, That whosoever looketh on a woman to lust after her **hath committed adultery with her** already in his heart."

Ladies, if we wear things that cause a man to lust after us, we are committing adultery *with* that man. God said it Himself. Women want to push the blame solely on the men. You have heard comments like: "They should keep their eyes to themselves," "Dirty old men," or "That's their problem." Yes, they should keep their eyes to themselves, and perhaps they could if we were not dressing so suggestively – so ungodly. We make our problem their problem when we parade around our community half-naked as if we do not receive enough attention at home. Ladies, God created men to desire women. We want men to keep their desires in check; therefore, we must keep our attire in check. We do not have to be flamboyant and indecent in our dress.

The Discussion

1. *Is it wrong for women to look beautiful?*

Indeed not! God created beauty. He made women beautiful. Many women are described in the Bible as beautiful or fair. Several examples from Scripture of beautiful women are:

A. Sarah	**- Genesis 12:14-15**	**- "very fair"**
B. Abigail	**- 1 Samuel 25:3**	**- "a beautiful countenance"**
C. Esther	**- Esther 2:7**	**- "fair and beautiful"**
D. Rachel	**- Genesis 29:17**	**- "beautiful and well-favored"** (outward beauty, but not inward)
E. Bathsheba	**- 2 Samuel 11:2**	**- "very beautiful"** (misused her beauty)
F. The Proverbs 31 Lady		**- (inward and outward beauty)**

Since God created beauty, He wants us to look our best for Him; after all, we are daughters of the King. Psalms 45:13 acclaims, "The king's daughter *is* all glorious within: her clothing *is* of wrought gold." This verse speaks of both an inward and an outward beauty. Beauty involves more than just outward appearance. We have probably all known someone who, though she was physically beautiful, had an ugly heart filled with sin and pride. Consequently, she was not beautiful at all.

You see, ladies, **balance is the key!** It is the key in all areas of life. When Jesus Christ lived on this earth, He displayed perfect balance in every area of His life. We will not be perfect in this life, yet we are to strive to be like Christ. A missionary to the Philippines once described balance as "right living." That is a tremendous definition. It is applying that which is right to your life. It is applying God's principles and coming up in the middle of the scale, just where God wants you. He does not want you to live lower than His standards or make up "new" standards that He did not set. He simply desires that we do what He says in His Word; that is application.

The balance on the "beauty" scale is balancing inward and outward beauty. God wants us to make our inward hearts beautiful for Him by daily reading of His Word, meditating and applying it to our lives, and daily praying. But, we are not to neglect our outward, physical appearance either, because that is what people see. We are King's daughters; therefore, we should look like it.

There are two indefensible trends in this area, and both are out of balance. The first trend is to be **worldly** in our dress, which as we have discussed earlier is sinful and out of balance. The second trend is to be **drab, dowdy, and unkempt** in our appearance. This, too, is wrong and out of balance. God desires that we be in the middle of His scale; that is perfectly balanced between maintaining standards of modesty and looking clean, orderly, and beautiful. Remember the Proverbs 31 Lady. She girded her loins with strength and honor through God's Word, and she clothed her family and herself with scarlet, tapestry, silk, and purple. What a lady! She had that balance.

Ladies, our goal in dress is to please Christ. Colors and pretty clothes are not wrong. God made colors and the resources to make fabric. We need not be drab and unbecoming, nor do we need to be immodest and look like ladies of the street. May we find God's balance and apply it to our lives in the area of beauty.

2. *Is it wrong to wear jewelry and makeup?*

No, balance is also the key in these matters. Dr. Bob Jones, Sr. once said, "If the barn needs painting, paint it." We would not let our homes or barns remain unpainted and drab, yet we sometimes allow our faces to be in such a state of disrepair. **The goal in wearing makeup is a natural look that enhances our face and eyes.** We want people to focus on our face, or countenance when they see us. We do not want them to run in fear when they see our pale, peaked face, nor do we want them to stare in horror at our over-painted, gaudy appearance. Moderation is the answer. Philippians 4:5 states, "Let your moderation be known unto all men. The Lord *is* at hand."

The key to balance in makeup and dress is to glorify God in everything that we do and to please the Lord Jesus Christ. Paul's exhortation in 1 Corinthians 10:31 addresses this in principle, "Whether therefore ye eat, or drink, or whatsoever ye do, do all to the glory of God." A meek and quiet spirit pleases Christ. Therefore, balance the outward man with natural looking makeup and the inward man with a meek and quiet spirit (1 Peter 3:3-4).

Lest someone argue that makeup and jewelry are wrong, here are some examples of proper jewelry and makeup in the Bible:

A. **King's Daughters** - Psalms 45 - This reference speaks of Christ and His throne. It tells us that His garments are fragrant with myrrh and aloes. Also, the king's daughters wear clothing of gold and fine needlework which are associated with Christ's kingdom. The Queen stands at His right hand in gold of Ophir.

B. **Rebekah** - Genesis 24:16, 22, 47, 52, 53 - She was a virgin and very fair to look upon. Jewelry was bestowed upon her as a blessing by Eliezer, Abraham's servant. Did she just thank him and hang it on the wall of her tent? No, she no doubt wore it!

C. **Job** - Job 42:11-12 - He was given earrings of gold for his family in his latter end as a blessing from God.

D. Proverbs 25:12 - An earring is considered a good gift; it is compared to wise reproof on an obedient ear.

E. **Jesus Christ** - John 12:3 - Of course, Jesus Christ did not wear makeup or jewelry; however, He allowed Mary to anoint His feet with ointment of spikenard, a costly, scented ointment. It was symbolic of His impending death.

Some will use the Scripture of 1 Peter 3:3 as an argument for not wearing jewelry. However, we need to look at this verse in its context. "Whose adorning let it not be that outward adorning of plaiting the hair, and of wearing of gold, or of putting on of apparel. . ." This verse would then mean we could not wear clothing either! Peter is instructing the ladies in the fourth verse that the most important quality to have is a "meek and quiet spirit." It is not wrong to braid the hair, put on jewelry, or wear clothing, but the most beautiful trait to possess is the "meek and quiet spirit" which, as we have seen, is indispensable.

There is also an improper example of jewelry and makeup in Scripture. Her name is Jezebel. She overdid it! Plus, she had a wicked heart. 2 Kings 9:30 speaks of how she painted her face. She possessed no balance in her life. She was wicked through and through.

Ladies, you must decide for yourself whether or not to wear makeup. Again, balance is the key. If you desire to wear it, do it naturally, not seeking to attract improper attention, but to look your best for the King. If you do not desire to wear it, it is certainly your prerogative not to, but do not look down upon those who do wear it. Remember that a meek and quiet spirit is of great price to the Lord.

The Decision

Dear lady, you must ultimately decide to obey God's laws of modesty or to reject them. It is a decision that comes from a heart that desires to be pure before God in spite of what the world is doing or wearing. It is not popular in this day and age to wear dresses. It used to be; however, those days are gone, probably never to return. We live in a world of compromise and apostasy. Will you have the courage to stand dressed in a manner becoming to a woman professing godliness? It positively matters to God what you wear. He is the Designer of clothes. He designed them to cover our nakedness that we may remain pure and holy before Him, before fellow believers, and before the world. Modesty truly is the heart of purity. Will you dress modestly and remain pure before your King?

Suggested Assignment

As you shop this week or pursue other activities, notice the ladies who are dressed modestly and those who are dressed immodestly. What drew your attention to the ones who were dressed immodestly? What part of the body did the immodesty draw attention to? *(Consider the principles of modesty we just discussed)*

Remove an immodest article of clothing from your closet and replace it with a modest piece.

Notes

Chapter 4

IDENTIFICATION

"The Heart of Femininity"

Most godly, Christian ladies may have no problem with the principle of modesty discussed in the last chapter. However, they often trip, become offended, and leave good Bible-believing churches over the next Biblical principle of identification found in Deuteronomy 22:5 and 1 Timothy 2:9-10.

Distinction in Creation and Make-up

According to Webster's dictionary, identification means "an act of being identified, the state of being identified, and the evidence of identity." In the matter of dress, God wanted to distinguish gender. We see this evidenced by creation when He made them male and **female**. God created us special and wanted us to be feminine (meaning, "characteristic of or appropriate or unique to women").

The Keil and Delitzsch Commentary states that Deuteronomy 22:5 was written "to maintain the sanctity of the distinction of the sexes which was established by the creation of man and woman." (Lackey)

We also see gender distinguished in the make-up of the male and female. God made man physically strong and woman the weaker vessel. Man is the leader; woman is the follower. In the family, it is man and wife. The family function is ordained with man as the head of the home. What caused these distinctions to change?

Distinction Erased

Man's fallen nature eroded the distinctions that God intended. Romans 1 tells us that as man became worse and worse, sins led to the debauched pattern of masculinity in women, femininity in men, transvestite lifestyle, cross-dressing, and homosexual sins. Man became so degraded that God gave him over to a reprobate mind. However, God did not change! We still see His will expressed throughout the Word of God to continue those distinctions. To avoid sameness and sinful tendencies, God commanded us to dress with distinction, to dress in such a way to identify our gender as determined by God.

Distinction Commanded

The Lord still commands distinction in marriage, in our roles, in our hair, and even in our dress. It is man and wife, Adam and Eve (not Adam and Steve, or Madam and Eve). The pastor is to be the husband of one wife. Women are to have long hair; men are to have short hair. Men are to dress like men, and women are to dress like women. We must be identifiable by our appearance.

Matthew Henry said there was a problem in Bible days with an idolatrous custom the Israelites were adopting. The pagan custom came from the Gentiles in their worship of Venus. Believe it or not, they were cross-dressing! Women were wearing armor and men were wearing women's clothing! God hated it! He wanted a distinction between the sexes, not cross dressing or androgynous clothing – clothing having the "nature of both male and female" or unisex clothing which almost totally makes up the wardrobe of today. When we as Christians accept these dress patterns, we are in violation of the Scriptures. "To break down the distinctions by incorporating characteristics of one gender into the clothing of the opposite gender is disobedience to God's Word." (Barry, p. 27)

Distinction in Wardrobe

Who wears what? What is man's distinctive clothing? What is woman's distinctive clothing? Do men wear dresses or skirts? NO! Should women wear pants? NO! In fact, wearing pants accents or draws attention to the pelvic and hip area of the lady, areas only her husband should see. A dress does not draw attention to this area unless it is too tight and formfitting. What then could we wear today that would be as different as possible from a man? A dress! Why are we afraid to be different and look like ladies from the front, back, and side? Subconsciously, are we trying to prove we are equal with a man?

What does the New Testament say? 1 Timothy 2:9-10 instructs us ladies to array ourselves with that "which becometh women professing godliness." "Becometh" means "suits." Have you ever asked yourself, "What 'becomes' or looks like a woman professing godliness?" Even the unsaved world knows what a woman is to wear as evidenced by the marking of public restroom facilities. The little man on the door is in pants; the little woman is in a skirt or dress. Distinction is universal. When we visited Chile, Brazil, Mexico, and Canada, these same symbols were used to indicate gender.

However, women in the 21st century make their arguments to justify their continued wearing of pants. But if their heart is tender to obey the Word of God, they will see the fallacy in their arguments. Let's examine a few.

Arguments

1. "That's Old Testament Law!"

In Bible days, there were three primary types of laws: civil, ceremonial, and moral. Civil laws dealt with a particular people, the Jews, during a particular time, and related to the nation and their social affairs. These laws involved "justice and equity, the protection of the innocent, the punishment of the evil-doer, human rights and property rights," etc. (Slemming, p. 51)

Ceremonial laws, on the other hand, involved rituals and sacrifices, citing ceremonies the Jews were to observe such as feasts and offerings. When a person broke one of these laws, it was said to be "an abomination or unclean to **you**." *(Lev. 11:10-12, 20, 23; Deut. 14:7, 10, 19)* These laws passed off the scene with the death and resurrection of Jesus Christ, as our ultimate sacrifice for sin. *(Col. 2:14)*

The only type of law remaining is that of the moral law. Noah Webster in his 1828 dictionary defined moral law as: "a law which prescribes to men their religious and social duties, in other words, their duties to God and to each other." This law regulated the individual life. Men have relationships with God, other men, and themselves. God gave Moses the Ten Commandments and many other laws to serve as the moral law to govern these relationships. Moral law was never eradicated. In fact the New Testament is even harder than the Old concerning moral law. If a man looks on a woman to lust, he has already committed adultery with her in his heart. The New Testament also teaches a hair standard differentiating men from women. The Ten Commandments (except for honoring the seventh day Sabbath) are still in effect for today as they were also part of the moral law. Deuteronomy 22:5 is not a ceremonial or civil law. Rather, it was/is a moral law still in effect today.

2. *"It's not that important."*

The Bible clearly states we are to dress like women and not like men. "The woman shall not wear that which pertaineth unto a man, neither shall a man put on a woman's garment: for all that do so are abomination unto the Lord thy God." *(Deut. 22:5)* Notice that word "abomination." What does that mean? The dictionary uses the terms "loathsome, extreme disgust, hatred." What was hateful to God then is still hateful to Him today.

It is an abomination! Unlike the ceremonial laws, broken

moral laws in the Old Testament were called an "abomination to the Lord." Deuteronomy 18:10-12 lists things considered an abomination to the Lord. Enchanters, witches, those using divination, wizards, and necromancers all were an abomination to the Lord. Are these things still an abomination to the Lord today? Yes! God still hates those things today!

Likewise, in Proverbs 6:16-19, we find seven more things which are an abomination to the Lord. In fact, the Scripture plainly points out that He hates, "a proud look, a lying tongue, hands that shed innocent blood, an heart that deviseth wicked imaginations, feet that be swift in running to mischief, a false witness that speaketh lies, and he that soweth discord among brethren." Does God still hate those things today? Yes!

What other things were an abomination to the Lord? Idolatry *(Deut. 7:25; 27:15)*, prostitution *(Deut 23:18)*, a false balance *(Prov. 11:1)*, a froward heart *(Prov. 11:20)*, lying lips *(Prov. 12:22)*, way of the wicked and thoughts of the wicked *(Prov. 15:9,26)*, pride *(Prov. 16:5)*, etc.

Isn't it interesting to note that God links wearing men's apparel with these abominations? Is wearing a pair of pants worth being loathsome to and detested by God? This is a very important topic to God. We must get it right.

3. *"They dressed differently in Bible times."*

This is correct; however, there was still a distinction in the apparel. Women's robes were longer and more decorative. The man's tunic could be long or knee length and was held to his waist by a girdle used for holding weapons or tools. *(1 Sam. 25:13)* When he needed freedom to work, he lifted the hem of his tunic and tucked it into his girdle, hence the phrase "gird up thy loins now **like a man** . . ." *(Job 38:3, 40:7)* A person could definitely tell who was a man and who was a woman by their clothing.

In Exodus 28:40-42, God gave specific instructions to Moses about the priests wearing breeches. They were to have their nakedness (the thigh) covered when offering sacrifices. Nowhere throughout the Bible do we find any Scripture commanding a lady to wear breeches. From this Scripture, we see that pants are a symbol of authority. Perhaps that is why the priests were commanded to wear them. They were the religious leaders of the day!

"Katastole" is the Greek word for apparel in 1 Timothy 2:9. This word means a long flowing garment that is let down. That leaves out pants as they are not long flowing garments that are let down! This word also eliminates shorts, mini-skirts, bathing suits, etc.

4. *"God looks on the heart, not the outward appearance."*

Many use the Scripture in 1 Samuel 16:7b, "for the Lord seeth not as man seeth; for man looketh on the outward appearance, but the Lord looketh on the heart." However, they really verify the importance of dress by this argument. Since man sees only our outward appearance and our goal is to reach and influence people for Christ, our outward appearance **is** important.

How do men expect a football player to dress? How do men expect a firefighter to dress? How do men expect a sailor to dress? How do men expect a preacher to dress? Each of these people have certain clothing which identifies their profession. Likewise, the Bible has given us guidelines to identify us as godly, Christian women. Really, a lady can dress any way she wants as long as she does not want to profess godliness as described in 1 Tim. 2:9-10 and does not mind being an abomination to the Lord. However, if she wants to be known as a godly woman, she will gladly identify her gender by her dress to please her God.

5. *"That's legalism."*

Legalism adds to salvation. "Theological legalism is a strict adherence to the law to bring or keep salvation." (Allison, p. 16) Dressing correctly does not save a person or keep him saved. Only confession of sins and believing on the Lord Jesus Christ saves a person and gives him eternal life. Therefore, a dress standard is not legalism. It is simply an obedient heart to a Biblical command. God says, " . . .ye shall therefore be holy, for I am holy." *(Lev. 11:45)* "But as he which hath called you is holy, so be ye holy in **all manner** of conversation; Because it is written, Be ye holy; for I am holy." *(1 Peter 1:15-16)*

6. *"I cannot do all I do in a dress or skirt and remain modest or warm."*

You may ask, "How do you shovel snow? Roof a house? Ride a bicycle or a horse?" There is a way to solve the problem with attractive culottes—a divided skirt, not gauchos or walking shorts. Remember our goal is to look like a lady from all sides.

Perhaps God did not mean for us as ladies to do all of these activities either. We should stick to ladylike activities. If we cannot look like a lady and do the activity, we should not do it. We should let Bible commands and principles determine our activities. Thermal underwear, leg warmers, knee socks, etc. can be worn beneath long skirts for warmth. Most of our excuses are really just excuses not to obey what God says in His Word. We are just afraid to "look different."

If a job demands a certain type of dress, you can make an appeal to your employer and explain that you are a Christian and want to dress like a lady. If he will not heed the appeal, then switch jobs. Most employers will be understanding and cannot afford religious discrimination. Let Biblical truth guide your decisions of jobs, activities, **dress**, etc.

7. *"But I like my pants for convenience and comfort."*

In our study of the history of dress, we discovered that many women wore pants for comfort or convenience. But comfort or convenience should not be a Christian lady's basis for her dress standard when the Word of God plainly commands what we as ladies are to wear. Where would we be eternally if Christ would have used comfort and convenience as a measure as to whether He should go to the Cross or not? No, He did not look forward to going to the cross, but He did it in obedience to His Father's plan in order to please Him. We should do the same with our dress. We need to be willing to accept God's limits on our appearance and comfort. Besides, pants in truth **are not** more comfortable than a dress.

Often, we dress for convenience. In 1 Kings 12:28, we see Jeroboam making worship convenient. He made calves of gold for the people and told them he realized it was too far for them to travel to Jerusalem to worship. Therefore, he made idol worship more convenient than worshipping the one true God. Dennis W. Costella said, "Jeroboam made worship convenient, but certainly not correct." Is that how it is with our dress, convenient but not correct according to Bible standards?

8. *"I wear only dress slacks without a front zipper. I think they are more modest than some skirts or culottes or dresses."*

You still break the principle of identification as found in Deuteronomy 22:5. Remember the word for apparel in 1 Tim. 2:9 meant a long and flowing garment. Slacks do not fit that category. The reason many women think slacks are more modest is because they have seen Christian ladies in their culottes sitting like a man and revealing their thighs, or they have seen Christian ladies in dresses without slips revealing more than a lady in a pair of pants. We need to use some common sense and realize a long flowing garment does not mean it is modest unless we take the other appropriate measures, i.e. sitting like a lady, wearing slips, etc. *(See Chapter 3 on modesty)*

Also remember that God has set two limitations on us—modesty and identification of gender. We can be modest and fail identification. Likewise, while a mini-skirt identifies gender, it fails the modesty test.

9. "No one will tell me what I can and cannot wear."

This truly is the heart of the matter of femininity. Our obstinacy in dress is really a submission problem. If we will not yield to God in this matter, what other commands are we disobeying? Jesus said, "If ye love me, keep my commandments." *(John 14:15)*

Will you be open and sensitive to the Holy Spirit's dealing in your life concerning the principle of identification? He is looking for you to surrender your heart and will to His will. Remember, God looks on the heart! Rejoice in the fact that God made you a woman! Be willing to identify yourself as a godly Christian lady who is unashamed to look like a lady! "But which becometh **women professing godliness** with good works." *(1 Tim. 2:10)* Hurrah for femininity! Be unique!

Suggested Assignment

When you go shopping this week, notice the number of ladies in a dress. Try wearing a dress or skirt sometime every day this week and notice others' reactions.

Notes

Chapter 5

WORLDLINESS

"The Heart of Friendship"

Worldliness – what a concept! It is a principle that is clearly taught in the Word of God, yet its terminology seems foreign to many of today's believers. Think about the downward steps that Christianity has taken toward worldly fashions in the last fifty to one hundred years. Many can probably remember when grandma did not and would not wear pants! She would not have worn short or tight clothes either. In the not too distant past, conformity to this world and its fashions was considered taboo for the Christian. Believers marked boundaries for themselves that they would not cross. However, today the trend is to be like the world—to accommodate them at all costs, to appear open-minded, to breakdown the walls between right and wrong. Believers try to look like, act like, smell like, sound like, talk like, think like, and dress like those who are lost and without Christ. Heaven forbid that they be *different*! [sic] Nonetheless, difference from this world is precisely what God expects, yea demands of His children. He desires that they look like, act like, and be like His only begotten Son, Jesus Christ. After all, He is the believer's divine example, and He completely abstained from worldliness.

The Definition

Perhaps you are asking yourself, "But what exactly is worldliness?" The word worldliness is derived from the word, *world*. In the Greek, the word is *kosmos* meaning "the sum total of the material universe and everything that belongs to it; the sum total of persons living in the world." (Bauer) *Webster's 1828 Dictionary* defines worldliness as "a predominant passion for obtaining the good things of this life; covetousness; addictedness to gain and temporal enjoyments." The world represents all that is hostile to God and His holiness. It is that which is sinful, ruined, and depraved. Therefore, Christians should stay away from all forms of worldliness, including worldly dress.

The Determiner

What is the determiner of worldliness? Worldliness is determined by the Word of God. Believers must use the Bible to determine their faith and practice. God's Word is the divine authority by which we must live our lives. 2 Timothy 3:16-17 declares,

> "All scripture *is* given by inspiration of God, and *is* profitable for **doctrine**, for **reproof**, for **correction**, for **instruction in righteousness:** That the man of God may be perfect, throughly furnished unto all good works."

The Bible teaches, reproves, corrects, and instructs us in God's perfect ways. It is inspired, inerrant, and infallible; therefore, we have a responsibility to obey it. When the Bible tells us as ladies that there are principles of separation, modesty, identification, and worldliness, we are responsible before God to obey them.

The Dogma

Though God commands Christians to separate from the world and conform to His holiness, believers everywhere seem to be "buddying-up" with the world. Instead of heeding Romans 12:2 not to conform to the world, Christians completely bypass this command to blend into our deteriorating culture. The cry today is to be like sinners so as not to offend them. Many well-meaning Christians actually believe that they must be like the world in order to win them; thus, they act just like the lost. They go to the same places as the world, drink the same liquor, listen to the same music, and dress the same way. Though God calls for a difference in dress through the principles of modesty and identification, many Christians prefer to wear this world's fashions. After all, no one wants to look like an oddball or be different. Yet, God calls for His born again children to abstain from worldliness and conform to His image for several reasons.

First, how will sinners know that they need a Savior when believers look and act just like them? God demands a difference between the saved and the unsaved to show sinners their need of a Savior and forgiveness of sins. It would seem foolish for one zebra to tell another zebra that he needed to change his stripes if they both looked exactly alike. The same is true of believers. The world knows precisely what Christians should act, look, and dress like. They expect it of them, too. The problem is that God's children convince themselves that they need to act like the world and be "cool." It is a no win situation. Sinners are looking for a difference that is simply not evident, and believers are fooling themselves into thinking that if they look like the world, they are fulfilling their obligation to it. That is part of the reason why so many unsaved people are calloused to the Gospel.

Secondly, God commands the separation of Christians from the world. There is no way to get around that command, except to blatantly refuse to obey God. Acting like the world places the believer at odds with God Almighty. Believers need to return to a holy fear of God and a determination to do right though it seems inconvenient.

Thirdly, God commands that believers make no friendship with this present world or its system of beliefs. The philosophy of this world dare not become the philosophy of God's children. We must be willing to swim upstream against the world's current.

The Defector

God's Word clearly forbids believers to make friendship with this present world. James 4:4 declares,

> "Ye adulterers and adulteresses, know ye not that **the friendship of the world is enmity with God? whosoever therefore will be a friend of the world is the enemy of God**."

God spells out quite clearly that you are either His friend or His enemy. There is no middle ground. You are either for Him or against Him. The word enmity means "the quality of being an enemy; the opposite of friendship; ill will; or hatred" *(Webster's 1828 Dictionary)*. For Christians to take the position of friendship with the world, they automatically defect from God's army, align themselves with the world, and consequently make themselves God's enemies. Perhaps they do not desire such a dreadful position, but they have placed themselves in it by refusing to separate and renounce friendship with the world. Though their salvation is secure, their fellowship with God is broken. Therefore, they cannot receive the abundant blessings that God desires to give them.

Many Christian ladies are allowing their worldly attire to hinder their friendship with Jesus. If they were asked if they desired to be God's enemy, they would certainly reply with an emphatic, "No." Yet, their dress automatically decides their position for them as a friend to the world, and therefore, His enemy in this area. They are failing to please the Lord and represent His Biblical model of dress. Ladies, it is dangerous to allow your wardrobe to hinder your relationship with Christ. It is time for ladies to stand up and declare their colors for Jesus in regard to dress.

The Devotion

1 John 2:15-17 states,

> "Love not the world, neither the things *that are* in the world. **If any man love the world, the love of the Father is not in him**. For all that *is* in the world, the lust of the flesh, and the lust of the eyes, and the pride of life, is not of the Father, but is of the world. And **the world passeth away**, and the lust thereof: but he that doeth the will of God abideth for ever."

God soundly declares that if believers love the world, they do not have God's love in them. Again, there is no gray area. You either love God and have His love in you, or you do not. It is so easy to be caught up in the things of this world because we constantly see them. That is why it is so essential to spend time with the Lord everyday through Bible reading and prayer. It alone gives us the right focus and the proper love for God that we need. If we truly love God, we will keep His commandments *(John 14:15*). This includes His commandments on dress.

These verses also state the true focus of this world. Since the entrance of sin in the garden, the world has been totally infiltrated with the lust of the flesh, the lust of the eyes, and the pride of life. Let's think about these categories of sins in regard to dress. We want to look like the rest of the world because of our pride, don't we? Perhaps we want to look sharp or sexy for others; that sin deals with the lust of the flesh both in our own lives and in men by causing them to sin in desiring us. Many times we ladies desire items of clothing that are not appropriate for Christians. This sin could be categorized as the lust of the eyes. As you can see, ladies, our worldly dress can cause us a lot of problems.

Someday this world and all that is in it is going to pass away. 1 Corinthians 7:31 states, "And they that use this world, as not abusing *it:* for the fashion of this world passeth away." It is time that we stop investing in the fashions of this world and invest in that which will last for both time and eternity. The word fashion in that verse is the Greek word *schema* which means "external conditions." Of course, that Greek word *schema* brings to mind the word, "scheme." This world with its fashion advertising is full of schemes that will entrap and ensnare us. They are all designed for one purpose—to distract our minds from pleasing Christ and winning the souls of men; that is, from what really counts and is lasting. While we ladies are fighting for the right to dress as we please, lost souls are dying and going to hell.

The Deceiver

There is one ruler over this world and its wicked system. He is opposed to God and all who stand for God's truth. Of course, he is Satan. 2 Corinthians 4:4 asserts,

> "In whom the **god of this world** hath blinded the minds of them which believe not, lest the light of the glorious gospel of Christ, who is the image of God, should shine unto them."

Satan is the god of this world. His goal for the world is to blind the unsaved from repentance. However, if he cannot keep people from salvation, his objective is to keep them trapped in the snares of this world. He desires to blind believers from doing that which is pleasing to Christ and is glorifying to His name. Jesus delights in the Christians obeying His Word.

Ladies, we cannot allow Satan to blind us from seeing the truth about dress. It *does* matter what we wear! What we do with worldliness (ie., embrace it or abhor it) is the heart of our friendship. If we do not choose to obey God and do His will in the area of dress, we are choosing to obey Satan and to be willing prey to his entrapments. It is time to remove the blinders and see the truth from God's Word.

The Dilemma

There is probably not a lady who will read this book that would dare to say that she desires to be Christ's enemy, that she does not want to show her love for God, or that she wants to be blinded by Satan. When we place things in that light, it seems easy to want to dress in a way that pleases God. But then we go out into the world and realize that it is not easy to change our dress or our ways. Because this generation "grew up" with ladies wearing pants, it seems normal. In fact, it probably rocks your world to think of changing it. Short skirts and shorts are fashionable and cool, not to mention the fact that everyone is doing it. In truth, we do not want to be the oddballs or look like old "fuddy-duddies" (though the Bible does call us a peculiar people). Plus, when you are used to wearing pants, they seem warm and comfortable (this author disagrees after changing from my skintight blue jeans). In addition, the allurements and peer pressure of this world sometimes seem too much for our frailties. The writer of the song, "I Must Tell Jesus," must have known the same wrestling for he states,

> "O how the world to evil allures me!
> O how my heart is tempted to sin!
> I must tell Jesus, and He will help me
> Over the world the victory to win."

If we were sincerely honest with ourselves, it comes down to the fact of "*I* want to do what *I* want to do." However, that does not absolve us of our responsibility to God or the unsaved world.

The Denial

Though it is not easy to admit that we have been mistaught, we must change our wardrobe, and do right, God calls for His children to follow Him. Luke 9:23 expounds,

> "And he said to *them* all, **If any *man* will come after me, let him deny himself, and take up his cross daily, and follow me**."

Christ tells us that if we truly want to follow Him, we will have to deny ourselves some of the pleasures of this world. Christ denied Himself the splendors of heaven and fellowship with His Father for 33 ½ years. He came to this earth knowing that men would reject, revile, spit upon Him, and ultimately kill Him on a cruel, wooden cross. In light of that fact and the fact that He bought us with His own precious blood, He has the right to tell us to deny ourselves a few things. Giving up a pair of pants or shorts is not going to bring us the tremendous suffering of the cross. Aren't we as human beings selfish to desire all of the creature comforts at the expense of our fellowship with the One who gave His very life for us?

The Death

Ephesians 2:1-3 proclaims,

> "And **you *hath he quickened,* who were dead in trespasses and sins**: Wherein in time past ye **walked according to the course of this world, according to the prince of the power of the air**, the spirit that now worketh in the children of disobedience: Among whom also we all had our **conversation in times past in the lusts of our flesh, fulfilling the desires of the flesh and of the mind**; and were by nature the children of wrath, even as others."

Jesus Christ has quickened us as believers. That means that we were dead in sin, and He made us alive again (*1 Cor. 15:22*). He made us alive through His death on the cross. Though vile, worthless sinners, He cleaned us and gave us value. Why then would we want to return to following the prince of the power of the air?

It calls to mind the pumpkin story that has been traveling around the email circuit. A woman was asked by a co-worker, "What is it like to be a Christian?" The co-worker replied, "It is like being a pumpkin. God picks you from the patch, brings you in, and washes all the dirt off of you. Then He cuts off the top and scoops out all the yucky stuff." He removes the seeds of doubt, hate, greed, *wrong dress*, etc… Why would anyone want to go back to the pumpkin patch after being all cleaned up?

Paul declared that he had to die daily to himself (*1 Cor. 15:31*). He also stated that his body required being brought into subjection to Christ. 1 Corinthians 9:27 declares,

> "But **I keep under my body, and bring *it* into subjection**: lest that by any means, when I have preached to others, I myself should be a castaway."

If Paul's body required subjection, ladies, how much more do our bodies require it? We must be willing to die to our desires and petty wants in order for Christ to live in us. Otherwise, we will be the castaways (disapproved).

The Decision

Romans 12:1-2 states,

> "I beseech you therefore, brethren, by the mercies of God, that **ye present your bodies a living sacrifice, holy, acceptable unto God, *which is* your reasonable service**. **And be not conformed to this world: but be ye transformed by the renewing of your mind**, that ye may prove what *is* that good, and acceptable, and perfect, will of God."

Ladies, the decision to change your dress, conform to the image and teaching of Christ, and renounce friendship with this world rests totally upon your shoulders. No one can make the decision for you; however, Christ is there to help you through it. He tells us that the presenting of our bodies to His service is reasonable. It is what we should do in light of what Christ has done for us. The process starts by deciding not to be conformed to this world and rejecting worldly philosophy. It continues through the renewing of the mind for Christ. This process takes place by reading God's Word, submitting to His authority, dying daily to self, and maintaining a time of prayer.

During his days as president, Thomas Jefferson and a group of companions were traveling across the country on horseback. They came to a river which had left its banks because of a recent downpour. The swollen river had washed the bridge away. Each rider was forced to ford the river on horseback, fighting for his life against the rapid currents. The very real possibility of death threatened each rider, which caused a traveler who was not a part of their group to step aside and watch. After several had plunged in and made it to the other side, the stranger asked President Jefferson if he would ferry him across the river. The President agreed without hesitation. The man climbed on, and shortly thereafter the two of them made it safely to the other side. As the stranger slid off the back of the saddle onto the dry ground, one in the group asked him, "Tell me, why did you select the President to ask this favor of?" The man was shocked, admitting he had no idea it was the President who had helped him. "All I know," he said, "is that on some of your faces was written the answer 'no,' and on some of them was the answer 'yes.' His was a 'yes' face."

Does your face say "yes" to God's friendship or does it say "yes" to the friends and fashions of this world?

Suggested Assignment

Seek the Lord and ask Him what worldly clothing He would have you remove from your wardrobe. When He shows you, will you be willing to obey?

Chapter 6

SURRENDER

"The Whole Heart of the Matter"

The Problem

Have you surrendered to God's friendship or are you still saying "yes" to the world? Our natural man wants to remain in control of things in our lives. That is why salvation is so difficult for many. It is accepting by faith that which we have not seen. After salvation, we begin to learn Biblical principles of separation and service. Why are the separation principles so difficult? Perhaps we have not surrendered or dedicated our whole life. One preacher called "surrender" the "missing link." Usually the order of our Christian walk is stated as saved – separated – serving. Applying the "missing link" of surrender, it should be saved – **surrendered** - separated - serving. In the proper order, principles of separation will not be difficult if we have surrendered to God.

What does that word surrender mean? Webster says it means "to yield to the power of another; to give or deliver up possession." Synonyms include: "submit, conform, yield, dedicate, succumb, defer, accede, lay down, humble one's self, bend, obey, **come to terms**, relinquish, give up, **abandon, part with**."

The Plea

In Romans 12:1-2, Paul actually begged or made a plea with the Roman believers to present their bodies a living sacrifice! He instructed them not to be conformed to the world, but to be transformed!

The springboard of duty and obedience is this matter of surrender. If we are totally surrendered, we will want to do anything and everything to please the Lord. We will not use carnal reasoning and arguments to exempt ourselves from an obvious Biblical truth.

What are we to surrender to Him? Our bodies, our minds, - our whole being! Notice that Paul did not **command** this. He **entreated** them. Christ wants our surrender to be a voluntary act – "a free-will offering." It is the **least** we can do after what Christ has done for us. "For ye are bought with a price: therefore glorify God in your **body** and in your **spirit** which are God's." *(1 Cor. 6:20)*

The Presentation

Once we voluntarily surrender or present our bodies as a living sacrifice, we are better able to apply Biblical principles of separation.

Paul himself knew the difficulty of mastering the body and the flesh, for he stated in 1 Cor. 9:27, "But I keep under my body, and bring it into subjection: lest that by any means, when I have preached to others, I myself should be a castaway."

Jesus told us that if we are going to follow Him, there are things that we will have to deny ourselves. When Jesus denied Himself the pleasures of heaven and died for us, the issue of denying ourselves a pair of pants really does not even begin to compare to His sacrifice. He was crucified for us; we must daily crucify our flesh to live for Him. Jesus said in Mark 8:34b, "Whosoever will come after me, let him **deny** himself, and take up his cross, and follow me." Galatians 5:24 says, "And they that are Christ's have **crucified the flesh** with the affections and lusts."

Likewise, Christ also submitted His will to God the Father. From His example, we see subjection, self-denial, submission, and ultimate surrender to the cross. In James 4:17, the Scripture says, "Therefore to him that knoweth to do good, and doeth it not, to him it is sin." When we know to do right and refuse to obey, God says that it is sin.

The Promise

Paul began his plea in Romans 12 beseeching the believers "by the mercies of God." What about those mercies? Psalm 86:5 says that God is "plenteous in mercy." Lamentations 3:22-23 tells us His compassions are new every morning. God will supply the mercy we need. If we present our bodies in surrender, Paul tells us we will prove "what is that good, and acceptable, and perfect will of God."

Don't you want to be in God's perfect will? Then apply the "missing link." Are you willing to voluntarily surrender your wardrobe to the Lord? To relinquish it? To abandon it? To part with it? Are you willing to wear what He would have you to wear? Is your body an "instrument of righteousness?" Can others see that Christ lives in you through this important area?

Perhaps this book has explained Biblical principles you have never heard of or been taught. Romans 12:2 says, "Be ye transformed by the renewing of your mind." Once your mind is renewed, there is to be a change, a transformation. You prove your love for God by obeying His known will for your life. Will you surrender and make that transformation? Will you bow your will to God's will? If your whole life is surrendered to God, He will have every part of your life including your dress. Won't you prove your love for Him by surrendering your whole will to Him including the issue of your dress? Remember, "to him that knoweth to do good, and doeth it not, to him it is sin." Will you apply the "missing link" of surrender?

"Whether therefore ye eat, or drink, or whatsoever ye do, do all to the glory of God." *(1 Cor. 10:31)*

"All to Jesus I surrender, All to Him I freely give;
I will ever love and trust Him, In His presence daily live.

I surrender all; I surrender all;
All to Thee, my blessed Savior, I surrender all.

All to Jesus I surrender, Humbly at His feet I bow;
Worldly pleasures all forsaken, Take me Jesus, take
me now.

I surrender all; I surrender all;
All to Thee, my blessed Savior, I surrender all."
(Judson W. Van de Venter)

Suggested Assignment

Continue to seek the Lord about your personal dress. Surrender parts of your wardrobe as He is faithful to convict your heart.

Chapter 7

TESTIMONIES

"The Heart of Surrender"

As stated in the foreword to this book, each year we have ladies classes at our church on this topic of dress and appearance. After we lay the Biblical groundwork, we have ladies share their testimonies of how God has dealt with them personally and specifically in this area of their Christian walk. As they share, God reminds us that He deals with each of us as individuals in His timing and His way.

Each testimony shared encourages those ladies, who have taken that step, to maintain the standard of dress. Likewise, each testimony reveals God's love and faithfulness to care enough to convict through the power of His Word. Listen as the following ladies share their personal testimony with you. Note God's perfect timing and methods in dealing with each precious lady. In each situation, the matter of surrender was involved. May these testimonies be an encouragement and a challenge to you in this matter of dress, the heart of surrender. (Each heading below is the testimony of a different lady)

A Lost Opportunity

God was patient with me. I chose to attend this church and place myself under its teachings. The matter of dress was all new to me and I did not understand. God gave me Proverbs 3:5-6 "Trust in the Lord with all thine heart; and lean not unto thine own understanding. In all thy ways acknowledge him, and he shall direct thy paths." It was like a light came on and God

began to convict me. I did not have to understand or lean to my own understanding.

I avoided fellowship with people and would run and hide in Wal-Mart if I saw one of the church women. No one ever apologized to me for the way they were dressed. They were not ashamed of wearing a dress and I was convicted.

I especially missed a wonderful opportunity of fellowshipping with an elderly lady in our congregation and all because of a "piece of material." (I knew the elderly lady always wore dresses.) Now that opportunity is lost forever as she has gone on to meet the Lord. I will not ever be able to make that up.

When I made the decision to change my dress, I was pregnant and nothing fit, so I sacrificed little. I began finding clothing and God used people to give me clothing in my size. I still go outside and garden. I use aprons to cover my better clothes.

It's not only what you wear or what Pastor says. It's **God's holiness** – Who He is, what He means to me, and what I should be doing in comparison to Him! I'm still learning. I challenge you to get off the fence; it's just not worth it!

A Difficult Struggle

I was not raised in a submissive family. My husband and father-in-law would always talk about dress. My husband told me, "You will wear a dress and get rid of your pants." I said, "I will not!" They were **my** pants. I always thought women had their pants and men had theirs.

We were not living for the Lord and our marriage was not good. One day I went forward in church. I do not even remember what the sermon was about. It was like the Lord picked me up and took me forward. I rededicated my life to the Lord. I asked Him to forgive me and make me to be what He wanted me to be.

One of my hardest things was to give up my pants. When I changed my dress, the Lord helped me change in other areas, too. You can go home and throw away all of your pants, and it may not be in your heart. It needs to be a decision from your heart! The Lord gave me this verse in 1 Thessalonians 5:24, "Faithful is he that calleth you, who also will do it."

A Cowgirl and A Tomboy

Before I was saved, I worked for a Christian boss. His wife wore dresses all the time. He tried to explain it to me, but I just did not understand.

Upon becoming saved, I started attending an independent, fundamental Baptist church. The ladies had classes and I picked up a book and a tape from these classes. I read the book and listened to the tapes.

Up to this point in my life, I was a cowgirl who wore jeans all the time and rode horses. When I saw the Scriptures, the Lord dealt with me and I decided to change. My lost husband would say, "How are you going to ride horses and not wear pants?" I told him I would deal with it when the time came. I knew there were feminine-looking culottes available. Then he would say, "You have to wear pants then to stay warm!"

I did not let his questions deter me and promptly got rid of all my pants. I had hardly any dresses at all, but the Lord provided finance for clothing. My decision has given me an opportunity to teach my children and to witness to others. I feel more feminine now, and do not miss my pants at all.

A Gradual Acceptance

I did not understand, and it was not for me! Why were pants man's apparel? I grew up in the 70's and **everyone** wore pants. When I was 13, we started attending an independent, fundamental Baptist church. It was there I heard for the first time a lady should not wear pants. I thought it was ridiculous! How could you ski, do any sports, etc?

I did not realize then that a man's thinking pattern is different from a woman's. I never thought of how I looked in something to a man. Why would a man think like that? I do not know if I was "bull-headed" and perhaps did not want to understand.

When God deals with us, Satan will be right there telling us, "That's impossible. There is **no** way. You will never be able to do that, **never!"**

God helped me to understand. I first heard the Biblical principles when I was 13, but never changed until I was 18. I prayed for God to help me understand.

A lady at Bible College explained that pants have a dividing line, a seam that cuts you in half. This reveals your shape and not your face. It was like something finally clicked in my mind. God helped me understand after five years of trying to understand on my own. It was like "night turned to day."

Satan will try to make it seem harder than it really is. How hard is it to go to your closet and put a skirt on every day? Do not let Satan tell you that you cannot do it!

Pleasing Man or Pleasing God?

I made a profession of faith when I was seven years old. At fourteen, I noticed other people who really had a desire to talk to God and read their Bibles. They had a deep love for the Lord. I realized I was not saved and accepted Christ at that time. It took me looking at someone else's life, seeing them give a testimony, and watching them live it to affect my own life for the Lord. So it was with dress.

I never heard of wearing skirts or dresses until I came to this church. I was not brought up that way. We wore pants and casual dress to church. No one said anything about it, and it just did not matter.

My reaction to women wearing dresses was, "No way! Why should I have to wear that? They are judging me!" I felt like everyone was looking at me when I wore pants. My reaction was rebellion. I imagined that women who wore dresses thought they were better than I was.

The Lord worked on my heart. He asked me, "Can you think about it?" Pastor would not even be talking about dress. He would deal with submission or some other topic and the Scriptures would stick in my heart. I thought, "I'm being submissive in every other area but this one. I will not even give this one a chance!" The Lord kept working in my heart with messages not even pertaining to dress.

I struggled a lot with pleasing man or pleasing God. So, my first decision was, "I'll wear skirts outside, but I'll wear pants when I go away." That way I would please man **and** God. Then I decided to wear skirts all the time, but I did not really have the conviction. Still I remained unhappy and did not have a peace in my heart. Finally, I determined to give it all to the Lord and asked the pastor's wife for Scripture on the topic.

She gave me several Scriptures and showed me that women dressing like men were an abomination to the Lord. I did not want that! I thought, "I would not want lying in my life – that is also an abomination." So, I decided to act on faith and obey, even though I did not have complete understanding. The Lord later gave me Proverbs 3:13, "Happy is the man that findeth wisdom, and the man that getteth understanding." I was not happy until I yielded to the Lord. Now I have peace.

Choosing God's Way *(A senior saint)*

I grew up in a non-Christian home, but my father always believed girls should wear dresses. The only time we ever wore pants was when we wore his overalls to work in the fields. I always liked the idea of girls in dresses.

When I married, I always wore dresses, even in the fields to work. I would go to the stores and see the backsides of women and think, "Pants do that to women." *(ie., reveal their backsides)*

Then, men designers began making "feminine" pantsuits, but they were still pants. However, it was something a man would not wear. I thought, "Now, I could wear that." So, I began wearing pants at home, but not to church.

We changed churches and the church was trying to reach the younger generation, so I began wearing pants to church along with everyone else. I thought they were feminine looking; however, I did not see the backside of me!

One day the pastors decided we needed to look more professional, so they asked the ladies to wear dresses. That's what **they** wanted, but was it what God wanted? I thought, "They don't have any authority to tell me what to wear!" I decided if my husband asked me to wear dresses then I would. However, I ran a day care center and I knew he could see the importance of wearing slacks in bending over and taking care of the children. I continued wearing pants.

Then we moved to a different location. My grandchildren began attending a Christian school and the rule was no pants on the girls. I could agree with that. Then the pastor asked us not to wear pants when we picked up the children from school. I could go along with that, but I continued to wear pants.

After our move, we went to a different church and had a new pastor. He preached on ladies wearing men's apparel. I thought, "This is still man's opinion," until he plainly showed us from the Bible. I said to myself, "If that is what God wants, then that is what I want." My desire was to please the Lord. It took me all of these years. I have chosen to do it God's way.

My Way, Not God's

I did not grow up in a Christian home and lived the first 34 years of my life not knowing Christ as my Savior. At that point I received Christ and I knew, WITHOUT A DOUBT, that I had a home in Heaven. But what do I do until then?

The Lord led our family to an independent, fundamental Baptist church through receiving a newsletter from that church. I wanted to attend a Baptist church because that was the kind of church I attended as a child, and I liked the pastor's name of this new church. *(Starr)*

We went to our first service on a Sunday morning and liked what we heard. We soon became faithful to all of the services, and I began to get to know the ladies of the church. There was an announcement of a discipleship class for new Christians. I was excited. I was so hungry for God's Word and wanted to grow spiritually!

I went to the first discipleship class with my notebook, pen, and Bible in hand ready to learn the first steps of Christianity and how I was to live my life so that it was pleasing to the Lord. The subject of dress came up. Everyone was talking about how Christian ladies are to dress modestly, and this did not include shorts, pants, tight clothing, and dresses and skirts should be at least knee length. Well, I have to tell you, I thought they were crazy! I raised my hand and said, "Excuse me, but what is wrong with wearing pants?" The teacher told me his wife would discuss it with me later. She did so, but I wanted no part of it. Even though she showed me Scriptures in the Bible regarding dress and modesty, it just did not "suit me" to believe this.

That summer, I attended the classes for ladies held by the pastor's wife. One of her classes was on (you guessed it) modest apparel for ladies! She even had one of the ladies bring in different types of modest culottes and several ladies gave their testimonies on how the Lord had worked in their hearts and convicted them about the way they were dressing. I sat there and listened intently, but my attitude was, "Yeah, yeah. . .whatever." She also shared many of the same Scriptures that had previously been shared with me in the discipleship class. I convinced myself that the Lord did not care how I was dressed. As a matter of fact, I became rather prideful of the fact that I **did** wear pants, and "did not care who knew it." My thought was, "If these ladies want to wear dresses all the time, that's fine with me, but I'm a Christian too and I'm willing to try my best to live the Christian life . . . but **not** in this area."

For the next three years I continued to be faithful to all the church services and made a lot of new friends with the ladies of the church. I even attended all of the discipleship classes again and the ladies classes in the summer. I was growing spiritually. So why was this area of dress such a big deal? It was bugging me. I spoke to many ladies in the church on this subject. Although I did not realize it at the time, I think I was trying to get them to "see things my way." But nobody did. Several ladies had even suggested to me that the Lord was working on my heart in this area because I always wanted to talk about it. Of course, I denied that.

Then it happened! I was getting dressed one morning to go to Vacation Bible School and was in my normal routine of the morning when suddenly the Lord spoke to me about my disobedience to Him in the area of modest dress. I had never considered it disobedience before. Why suddenly was I willing to listen and submit? Honestly, I just sat there and cried. When the Holy Spirit speaks to you, you know it, and believe me he was speaking to my heart . . .loud and clear! I realized that what everyone had shared with me before was true, and it was my pride and disobedience that kept me from seeing the truth. I couldn't wait to get to VBS that day. I remember I had to hold back tears as I shared the news with some of the ladies I was closest to. I believe I even saw tears well up in their eyes! Before I left my house that morning, I had gathered up all the pants and immodest clothing I could get my hands on at the moment. I took them to the church and asked a friend if she would "take my garbage out" for me. She was more than happy to do it. I had to give her several "loads of garbage" that week. I did not trust myself to hold on to them until later.

Almost a year has passed since my decision to be obedient to the Lord and dress in a way pleasing to Him. I did not expect the attacks that Satan has launched at me trying to get me to reverse my decision.

For the first few months, it was not a problem. However, I accepted a nursing position at a local hospital where all the nurses wore pants. I could remember the time when that was **my** working attire. As I shopped around for white uniform dresses, skirts, and culottes, I became very discouraged. Satan almost convinced me that the dresses and skirts were old-fashioned and that nurses just do not dress like that anymore. As I tried on dress after dress, I was very discouraged and thought that I just looked terrible and maybe the pants would be okay "just to wear to work." Somewhere along the way, the Lord kept me from giving in to this temptation and lie that Satan was trying to make me believe. I went ahead and bought several dresses and skirts. Still, though, I was not happy with how I looked.

One day as I was working and feeling like I looked ridiculous in a white nursing uniform, one of my patients told me that I was the only nurse on the floor who actually **looked** like a nurse. The Lord knew I needed to hear that. That has been one of the many positive comments that people have made about the way I dress. A co-worker said to me, "You always look like such a lady." I have also noticed that several of the other nurses I work with have started to wear dresses and skirts too!

I do not regret my decision at all. My disobedience and pride kept me from seeing things God's way. It does not matter whether or not we "agree" with what God has to say, we still need to obey Him. Deuteronomy 22:5 tells us that a "woman shall not wear that which pertaineth unto a man . . . all that do so are abomination unto the Lord thy God." It is so easy for us to tell ourselves that this is Old Testament and no longer pertains to us, but, if God hated it then, He hates it now because God **never** changes. He is always the same!

Other Comments

"I have attended Baptist churches for years and never heard this teaching before! Where has it been? Thank you for teaching me!" *(This lady immediately converted her whole wardrobe upon hearing the teaching.)*

"I don't understand it, but I am not going to let a pair of pants keep me from what I have found in the Lord."

"Men even treat me more like a lady and hold the door for me at the store."

"I just want to tell you thank you for inviting me to the classes that you had. I really learned a lot and am still learning. Please keep me in your prayers on dress. You opened my eyes on what the Scriptures says about how to dress."

"I noticed I received better treatment as I dressed and acted more like a lady. Doors were held. More help was offered with loading the car and I just felt pleased myself. God was showing me the way. Now, I no longer have to run and put on a skirt when the preacher comes because I have learned to obey God's Word, listen to the Holy Spirit, and understand what the Bible says about women looking and dressing like women."

"Now I realize that modesty was the first step. Yes, I have a true desire to look feminine and I believe dresses are the piece of attire God would have me wear to do that. I am diligently trying to model what is "shamefaced" and modest in front of my precious daughters. I need to rework **God's way** as over the years they saw me demonstrate **my way**. I still struggle. My husband is constantly helping me to evaluate my dress. It is a constant growing."

Suggested Assignment

If the Lord has personally dealt with you through the Biblical principles in this book, be sure to tell someone about it. Write out your testimony below to further enhance your new commitment.

Chapter 8

PROVISION
"The Heart of Trust"

Perhaps the Lord is convicting your heart about dress and total surrender to His perfect will through the principles and testimonies set forth in this book; nonetheless, you may also feel a little overwhelmed by the whole concept of change and its implications. After all, it means giving up certain garments in your wardrobe. For some, it may mean replacing an entire wardrobe. Thoughts may trouble you like, "My husband is not going to be happy when I tell him that I need a completely new wardrobe." Or, "my family will think that we have gone off the deep end." It is possible that not everyone will be happy with your choice to change. Despite the opinions of others, God will be extremely happy that you are choosing His way. He will bless you for your obedience to His Word. If God has convicted your heart, He will provide you with the necessary clothing to conform to His image.

The Contribution

When God convicts His children regarding an area of surrender, He is ready, willing, and able to provide the necessary materials to exact that change. After all, He is still the same Jehovah-Jireh of Abraham's day (Jehovah-Jireh = *the Lord will provide* - Genesis 22:7-14). Just as Abraham needed faith and trust in God to provide a ram for the sacrifice, so it is with us today. Abraham did not see the ram before he followed God's instructions to head up to Mt. Moriah and offer a sacrifice, yet God saw and was pleased with Abraham's trust in Him and thus fulfilled the required animal for the sacrifice. God is surely pleased when we step out in faith believing that He will provide for our needs. If you truly desire His will, He will provide modest, feminine clothes for you to wear. Step out by faith and trust Him.

God will provide you with clothes. Pray and ask God to supply you with proper clothing. He may provide in any of several ways. If finances are not a problem for you, stores are a good source for new clothes. It is not necessary to pay the full price for them. Wait for sales. Newspapers carry coupons for some major chains. End-of-season sales are a tremendous way to acquire modest clothes at a reasonable price. Buy clothing at a store that fits your pocketbook. Do not go to Macy's looking for clothes if Wal-Mart better suits your budget. It is best to avoid trendy clothes and fads. Build a wardrobe that will stand the test of time. Develop a base of clothes in neutral colors, and build the vibrant colors into your basic wardrobe. This will save you much money and many regrets of, "I am really sorry that I bought that."

If you cannot afford to buy all of your clothes from a store, consignment shops are a good source for new and used clothes. Look for bargains. Do not pay almost the same price for used clothes that you would pay for new ones, especially if they were on sale. Find a consignment shop that offers nice clothes at bargain prices. Yard sales are also a good place to look for clothing, especially children's clothes. If you do not sew, contact a good seamstress (perhaps right in your own church), and have her make you some culottes, jumpers, or skirts.

God knows your heart and your budget. If you simply cannot afford to buy any new or used clothes, God will provide you with them in miraculous ways. Maybe He will lay it on the heart of someone to give you clothes, hand-me-downs, or the money to buy them. Some churches and charitable organizations open their doors to the public to provide clothing free of charge. Whatever the method, God is up to the task if you are sincere and surrendered to His will. "Ask and ye shall receive."

The Clothes

Throughout the book, we have discussed **improper** types of clothing for women. Let's discuss what is **right** and **proper**.

Modest dresses, skirts, and culottes are proper dress for women. The basic criteria for them is that they fall below the knee and are not formfitting. There is a trend today that declares that culottes and straight skirts are wrong; therefore, these issues must be discussed.

When God declared that women should wear skirts and dresses, His standard was a long, flowing garment that is let down decently. He did not pronounce a specific measurement of material that is considered flowing. In other words, He did not say, "Three yards of material is required in each skirt to be considered flowing." However, He did give us common sense. Straight skirts that do not hug the body and show every bump or curve are considered modest apparel. Just be sure that your skirts do not hug your posterior section and that when you sit in a chair, it covers your knees. God did not tell us that we had to be draped with yards of curtain material in order to be modest. Use common sense in the matter. Be decent.

Culottes are considered decent if they are long and flowing garments. There are culottes that are truly culottes, and then there are culottes that are simply long shorts or gauchos. God does not want His children to wear shorts, not even long shorts. Nevertheless, if culottes are long, flowing and look like a skirt, they are modest and feminine. Some argue that the crotch makes them wrong and manly. If that were true, women should not wear underwear or nylons. If the crotch is not visible and the culottes look like a skirt, they are proper. God did not tell women, "Thou shalt not wear clothing with a crotch." The distinction between the crotch in culottes and the crotch in pants must be evident in order to be proper, modest dress. The crotch of pants is revealing and undisguised. Plus, it is tight to the body and formfitting. The crotch or inseam on culottes should be covered by flowing material and hang several inches below the pelvic area. If the seam of the culottes shows a dividing line, they are simply long shorts. Find a pattern for culottes that looks like a skirt. They are available. *(see p. 74 for information)*

Modest, loose fitting shirts, blouses, and sweaters are proper attire for a woman's torso. Be sure that the clothes are not glued to your chest. It is also important to wear modest undergarments. A lightly padded bra solves the problem of a woman's nipples sticking through her clothes. Again, a T-shirt under a light-colored blouse gives you extra protection. Be sure that you are not responsible for causing men to look at your chest.

The Checkup

In order to maintain a constant appearance of godliness and modesty, there are several questions that the Christian lady can ask herself in regard to her dress. It is advisable to check yourself in the mirror and perform an honest evaluation of yourself. Your husband may also provide you with honest opinions about your appearance.

The Criteria

The Bible gives us a clear criteria. Here are six questions that will help you:

1. Is it Modest? 1 Timothy 2:9-10
2. Is it Feminine? Deuteronomy 22:5
3. Is it Godly? Romans 12:2; 1 Cor. 7:31
4. Is it Appropriate? Titus 2:4 (sober = sensible)
5. Is it Beautiful? Psalm 45:13 (We are the King's daughters.)
6. Is it Exemplary? 2 Corinthians 3:2-5; 1 Timothy 4:12 (Others are watching us)

If our clothes pass this test, chances are that we will look like women professing godliness. God is pleased with a modest, feminine appearance. Are we an example to our children and to other ladies or are we causing others to stumble? Does our dress meet God's righteous standards?

The Crown

Now that you know the truth regarding dress and God's will for your appearance, what will you do with it? God Almighty tells us in His holy Word that knowing the truth will make us free *(John 8:32)*. Consequently, that truth must be applied to your life to make you free from the bondage of sin.

If you willfully refuse to obey God and His principles for your life, you will become stunted in your Christian growth. James 4:17 states, "therefore to him that knoweth to do good, and doeth *it* not, to him it is sin." Surrender your dress and wardrobe to God and allow Him to make you free and bless your life. Do not choose to live in rebellion to His precious Word *(1 Sam. 15:23)*. Decide today to follow God and His perfect ways. Then, commit yourself to "weeding out" that which is displeasing to Him in your wardrobe. Refuse to look back to your former fashions.

If you become discouraged, remember that God always rewards His own with blessings for faithful service. He will give you the strength to follow through with your decisions for Him. Read His Word, pray to Him for strength, and do right according to His holy ways. If you fall, get up and begin again. Commit your ways unto Him, trust Him, and He will bring it to pass (*Psa. 37:5*). You can have an appearance that pleases God and draws others to Him.

Suggested Assignment

If the Lord has touched your heart and you have made a decision after reading this book, feel free to share your testimony with us. Mail to the address on the order form on the last page. You may also want to order more copies of this book and share them with your friends or other ladies in your church.

Addresses for culottes:

1. **Christian Womanhood**
   8400 Burr Street
   Crown Point, IN 46307

   Phone – 219-365-3202

   These culottes are called the CW collection and look like a skirt in front **and** in back.

2. **Bird Publishing Company**
   1910 Edison Street
   Schererville, IN 46375

   Phone – 219-322-5523

   These culottes have a waistband with a yoke and are fully pleated. They are made from a simple four-piece pattern.

Sources

Allison, Mike. *Preaching Standards: Right or Wrong*? Shelbyville, Tennessee: Bible and Literature Missionary Foundation, 1984.

"Art, Design, and Visual Thinking," http://char.txa.cornell.edu.

"A Short Shorts Story," *Newsweek*, August 1, 1955, p. 29.

Barry, Richard. "Fashion Sense and Nonsense," *Faith for the Family Magazine*, May/June, 1985, pp. 26-28.

Bauer, Walter. *A Greek-English Lexicon of the New Testament.* (Revised by William F. Arndt, Frederick W. Danker, and F. Wilbur Gingrich) Chicago: The University of Chicago Press, 1979.

"Chronology – The History of Clothing," Internet.

"Clothes," *Saturday Evening Post*, June 26, 1920, p. 165.

Cloud, David W. fbns@wayoflife.org, May 9, 2001.

Cobb, Jane. "Girls Will Be Boys," *New York Times Magazine*, November 3, 1940, p. 10.

Corle, Cathy. *What in the World Should I Wear*? Claysburg, PA: "Revival Fires" Publishing, 1992.

Costella, Dennis W. "Pragmatism at the Cost of Fidelity," *Feature,* October-December 2002.

"Defense Styles," *Business Week*, August 2, 1941, p. 34.

Sources (continued)

Galyean, Eddie R. *Biblical Modesty*. Faith Baptist Publications, 1993.

Handford, Elizabeth Rice. *Your Clothes Say It For You*. Murfreesboro: Sword of the Lord Publishers, 1976.

"Hemline of Battle, "*Business Week*," April 18, 1942, p. 32-34.

Henry, Matthew. *Matthew Henry's Commentary*. Vol. I and VI Fleming H. Revell Company.

Johnson, David. "Timeline: Modern Fashion," factmonster.com.

Kent, Margaret. *How to Marry the Man of Your Choice*. New York: Warner Books, 1987.

Lackey, Bruce. "Bible Guidelines About Clothing," *O Timothy Magazine*, Vol. 9, Issue 12, 1992.

Lindsell, Harold, and Charles J. Woodbridge. *A Handbook of Christian Truth*. Old Tappan N.J.: Fleming H. Revell Co., 1953.

Martin, Curtis D., Ph.D. *God's Standard for Dress*. Fort Morgan, Colorado: Martin Publishing, 1995.

McDonnell, Eleanor Kinsella. "Fashion and the Hollywood Handicap," *The Saturday Evening Post*, May 18, 1935, p. 10.

"Paris Fashions," *Life*, November 20, 1944, pp. 47-49.

Sources (continued)

Presley, Beth Ann. "Fifty years of change: societal attitudes and women's fashions, 1900-1950," www.findarticles.com, Winter, 1998.

Roget's Thesaurus, P.S.I. Associates, Inc., 1987.

Slemming, C.W. *The Bible Digest*. Grand Rapids: Kregel Publications, 1960.

"Slit Skirts," *Life Magazine*, March 7, 1949, pp. 71-2.

Strong, James. *Strong's Comprehensive Concordance of The Bible.* Iowa Falls, Iowa: World Bible Publishers.

"The Case Against Clothes," *Newsweek*, December 11, 1944, p. 102.

"The History of Fashion and Dress," Week 14: WWI to WWII www.costumes.org., Online Version, University of Alaska at Fairbanks.

"Trousers in History," www.factmonster.com, The Learning Network Inc., 2001.

Ucef, Dr. Michael, www.leadingtheway.org.

"V for Voluptuous," *Newsweek*, September 6, 1943, p. 90.

Valentine, Elizabeth R. "Slacks," *The New York Times Magazine*, March 1, 1942, pp. 16-17.

Vine W.E. *Vine's Complete Expository Dictionary of Old and New Testament Words.* Nashville, Tennessee: Thomas Nelson Publishers, 1985.

Sources (continued)

"Wartime Living, Pants," *Time*, April 13, 1942, pp. 18-19.

Webster, Noah. *American Dictionary of the English Language*. San Francisco: Foundation for American Christian Education, 1828.

Webster, Noah. *Noah Webster's 1828 Dictionary*. Independence, Missouri: Christian Technologies, Inc., 1997.

Zodhiates, Spiros, Th.D. *The Complete Word Study New Testament*. Chattanooga, Tennessee: AMG Publishers, 1991.

How to Order

(Give a gift to your friends, Pastor's wife, teacher, relatives, or students and save $ in quantity.)

Additional copies of this book are available by mail.
Use the order form below and send to:

Starr Publications
740 Jefferson Lane
Red Lion PA 17356

Or, order online with credit card: www.Starr-Publications.com

Bookstores—Write and ask for a special discount Bookstore Order Form.

Clip, Complete, and Send with your check or money order

Order Form

Please send me:

Qty.	Title	Cost each	Total
____	***Women of the Bible, Vol. 5 Carnal & Conniving*** *New! Available October 25, 2005*	$6.60	$ ______
____	*Women of the Bible, Vol. 4 Powerful & Prestigious*	$6.60	______
____	*Women of the Bible, Vol. 3 Helpless & Hurting*	6.60	______
____	*Women of the Bible, Vol. 2 Faithful & Fruitful*	6.60	______
____	*Women of the Bible, Vol. 1 Helpmeets & Homemakers*	6.60	______
____	*Dress—The Heart of the Matter*	6.60	______

Subtotal A (add) $ ______

Less Discount for Quantity (circle one)......... - ______

3-6 bks 10% 7-12 15% 13-18 20% 19-45 25% 46-75 33% 76+ 36%

Subtotal B (subtract) .... $ ______

Add Shipping & Handling in USA by US Postal Media Mail + ______

1-3 bks $ 2.60 4-6 $ 3.10 7-9 $4 10-12 $5
13-16 $5.40 17-22 $.37 ea. 23-51 $.29 ea. 52+ $.26/bk

Order Total (include check or money order for…) $ ______

Please send book(s) to:

Your name ______________________

Mailing Address ______________________

City, ST, Zip ______________________

Phone # for questions ______________________

Send order to: Starr Publications, 740 Jefferson Lane, Red Lion PA, 17356